CURTAIN GOING UP!

The Story of Katharine Cornell

Curtain Going Up!

The Story of Katharine Cornell

BY GLADYS MALVERN

With a foreword by KATHARINE CORNELL

Julian Messner, Inc., New York

PUBLISHED BY JULIAN MESSNER, INC.

8 WEST 40TH STREET, NEW YORK

SEVENTH PRINTING MARCH 1949

PRINTED IN THE UNITED STATES OF AMERICA

BY MONTAUK BOOK MANUFACTURING CO., INC.

For
MY MOTHER

ACKNOWLEDGMENT

The author acknowledges source material from "I Wanted to be an Actress," the autobiography of Katharine Cornell as told to Ruth Woodbury Sedgwick, published by Random House, New York, 1938-9. Sincere gratitude belongs to Miss Gertrude Macy for her unfailing co-operation. I am indebted, also, to Miss Cornell herself who, bombarded with my questions, took the onslaught in her stride.

CONTENTS

FOREWORD

WERE ANYONE to ask me to summarize my career in the theater, I think I would be tempted to say: "Twenty-seven years of hard work." I suppose there may have been once, somewhere, an actress who became a success overnight, who sprang into public attention like Venus from her shell; there must be some basis in fact for a Cinderella legend so tenderly nursed for years. But if there is such an actress, I wouldn't know her or know of her; I've been too busy. Where there is work one loves and is determined to do well, there is contentment, which in turn fosters ambition to do even better. All over the world there are women who are doing hard work, who are striving to become finer, fuller beings moving apace with the events which condition them. Surely, many of these achieve serenity and have a relentless impetus to do better next time.

Among our women of tomorrow there may be some whom this account of an unfinished life will encourage in their desire to turn to the stage. There were many times in my youth when a friendly word would have meant all the difference, when I desperately needed the stimulus of encouragement. However, I was convinced that in this sort

of a career one cannot ask how to get started, how to go
about the business of being an actress. The whole secret lies
in finding out those things for oneself. To those who plan
to embark upon the hazards of a stage career or to those
who may be faltering, part way along it, the knowledge
that it can be done, that others have trod the same path
before, may prove helpful; I hope it will. But it will be
work—unglamorous, exhausting, dispiriting.

First of all, there must be a fierce determination, a deep
conviction that acting is the thing you must do; then there
must be a carefully planned series of assaults on a fortress—
the commercial theater—that is none too easy to storm.
Mere physical beauty isn't everything, but it is one barrier
less to climb over if you possess it. Intelligence, awareness,
sensitivity, self-effacement, industry—all these are necessary
in greater or less degree.

The picture of the American theater has changed, of
course, since I plunged into it in 1916. There is no longer
stock as I knew it: stock nowadays so often is a synonym
for the shoddy and second-rate, and it is confined to the
outskirts of large cities. The summer theater, which flour-
ished until wartime cut out vacationers and automobiles,
is no more. In New York, which still conditions the output
of the commercial theater of America, there has been no
modification of the dreary round of agents and producers
that was a vicious thing even a quarter of a century ago
when I went through it. Happily, however, there are not
only many more college and amateur groups throughout the
country today, but the quality and scope of their productions have also increased.

But perhaps young people who are considering a vocation, especially one in the theater, may find some inspiration in these pages, in which Miss Malvern has so accurately and sympathetically mirrored me and my career. No one can give you any formula for success: each must find his own path. For now more than ever, when footlights are dimmed in other lands, our own have need to shine the brighter, and new fuel must be added to the flame with which they burn.

PART ONE

ASPIRATION

CHAPTER ONE

ELEPHANTS

*I*N ALL the world there was no more active and fertile imagination than that of Doctor Cornell's little girl, Kit. For weeks now, ever since her father had told her that there was an act which had elephants in it coming to the Vaudeville Theater, and that if she were very good he would take her to see them, elephants had dominated her every waking moment.

"Will it be much longer before we go to see the elephants?" she asked each morning.

First the great event was two weeks off—and two weeks seemed interminable. Then there was only a week to wait; and then only a few days. Oh, she would be very good; and to this end she watched herself carefully, for it was unthinkable that the elephants would come to Buffalo and she should not see them.

"Is it tomorrow that we go to see the elephants?"

Mother laughed. "Yes, dear, it's tomorrow. Would you like to feed them?"

"*Feed* them?" Here was an added joy. Here was a joy so profound that it was almost incomprehensible. Here was an honor unsought—to be allowed to feed the elephants! "Me?"

3

"Yes. I'll tell Susie to fix you a bag of buns for the elephants."

"Oh!" gasped Kit, and lapsed into silence, for mere words profane moments so exquisite as this.

At last—at long, long last—the much-heralded day arrived.

They went in a streetcar. Too excited, too happy to talk, Katharine Cornell sat tensely beside her father, clutching the bag of buns which Mother had given her just before she left the house.

Almost everybody in Buffalo knew Dr. Peter Cornell, and now and then people boarding the car hailed him in friendly greeting; men with high collars and gray derbies, women with pompadours, their left hands bunching long skirts to save daintily ruffled hems from the dust, while their right hands held gay, lacy parasols—for in that year of 1903 no "lady" permitted herself the "vulgarism" of suntan.

The Cornells, related to Ezra Cornell who, in 1865, had founded the Cornell University at Ithaca, New York, were among the socially prominent families of Buffalo. Grandfather Cornell lived in a large, imposing frame house on a quiet, aristocratic street from which the house with an air of aloofness sat back majestically upon a wide and well-kept lawn. Behind it were commodious stables which even now Grandfather was talking of having converted into something called a "garage."

The young Peter Cornells, with their five-year-old daughter, Katharine, lived in a small frame house with a back yard, where Kit climbed fences. It was a pretty house of three stories with a veranda close to the street. Part of the first floor was used as Cornell's office, and a neat shingle nailed to the front porch read: "PETER CORNELL, M.D."

Riding beside her father now, Kit could close her eyes and actually see an elephant. Had the doctor suddenly asked his daughter what an elephant looked like, she could have told him all about it. An elephant was an animal, small and beautiful, something soft and furry, something which, perhaps, she might even be allowed to hold on her lap!

Elephants, she would have assured him knowingly, with that singular earnestness characteristic of the five-year-old, were wonderful. They came from faraway, story-book places; they belonged to the glorious, fabulous lands where Cinderella and Snow White and fairies lived.

"Well," announced her father, and behind his glasses his eyes were gay and bright as if he, too, were sharing in the wonder of that moment, "this is the place."

"Gonna feed elephants," declared his daughter, as he lifted her off the car.

"Yes," he agreed, and his voice sounded as if the pros· pect were as delightful to him as it was to her.

To the child the surroundings were all a colorful haze. Presently her father, to whose hand she clung tightly, led her inside the theater.

"I got seats in the stage box," he explained, "so you could get a good look at the elephants."

She nodded blissfully. The show began.

"Where are the *elephants?*" she queried worriedly.

"Ssh. They don't come on till the very end."

At length some enormous, gray, ugly creatures lumbered

into view. They had long, hideous tusks and huge flapping ears. Kit gave a little gasp of fright and nestled closer to her father.

"Those are the elephants," he whispered, his eyes on the stage.

There must, of course, be some mistake. "Those?" she asked, in a voice all suddenly atremble.

Still not looking at his daughter, he nodded.

Here, for Katharine Cornell, was disillusionment—stark, tragic, terrible. In that moment she was engulfed in a deluge of fear. She remembered the bag she was so carefully holding. No, no, never, never could she go near those dreadful creatures! She closed her eyes tight so as not to look at them.

"Well," declared her father at last, "it's over. Now they'll let us go on the stage and feed the elephants."

She opened her eyes to gaze up at him in mute and despairing appeal. She tried to speak, but words were impossible at the moment.

"Come on, Kit."

"I—I g-g-guess I—don't want to feed the elephants!"

His smile faded. "What?"

"I—I think I'd—just—l-like to—go home."

Surprised, questioning, her father stared down at her. Then he saw the agony of fear engraved upon that small, dark, sensitive face, and for a moment he hesitated. Doctor Cornell was a gracious host, a man of integrity, a jolly companion, but he was also a firm believer in discipline. Now, decisively, he reached down and took her hand, speaking in a stern, brusque voice.

"For a long time you've been talking about feeding those elephants. Now, you're going to feed them!"

"No!" she shrieked. "No!"

"I tell you, they won't hurt you. Come on."

Despite the child's shrieks of terror, he dragged her nearer and nearer to the elephants. Screaming, her small, thin body quivering, the child clung desperately to her father.

"No! No!"

Shrieking, sobbing, he led her to the stage. Now they were quite close to those leathery, enormous creatures.

People were staring. "That's Doctor Cornell and his little girl," a woman said. "My, such a scene! Such a scene she's making—in *public!*"

"Feed them!" her father insisted.

Her face livid, her small hand shaking, her dark eyes blurred with tears, the child opened the bag. Then suddenly, still screaming, she dropped the bag and ran off as fast as she could.

That was Katharine Cornell's first appearance on a real stage.

The Cornells were a gifted, colorful, energetic family with a flair for acting and an ingrained love of the theater. There were as yet no movies, but Buffalo was known among Broadway managers as a good "theater town." Having made a success in New York, plays were invariably sent on the road, and Buffalo was included in their itinerary. Added to this there were numerous amateur theatrical societies which were always in the process of play production, sometimes for their own enjoyment, but more often in the cause of some local charity.

From his youth, Grandfather Cornell had devoted his spare moments to this amusement. Play producing was his hobby, his delight, his unwavering interest, an enthusiasm which was shared wholeheartedly by his daughter, Lydia, and by his sons, Peter and Douglas. There was nothing that Grandfather Cornell enjoyed more than choosing a play, getting together an amateur cast, and directing it. His love for dramatics prompted him to fix up the attic of his large house as a theater, complete with curtain, lights, scenery and a stage. Here, at irregular intervals, his guests assembled in what was perhaps one of the first "little" theaters of America.

It was the directing, rather than the acting, which brought him most satisfaction. Had he listened to the glowing encouragement of his good friend, John Drew, he would have straightway exchanged his comfortable home in Buffalo for the hazards of a theatrical career, for John Drew, acknowledged to be one of the most distinguished stars in America, was voluble in his assertions that Cornell was a potential theatrical genius; but the elder Cornell had no desire for fame. He was having a glorious time producing plays for the sole enjoyment of himself, his family, his friends and his neighbors.

His son, Peter, even as a boy spent every spare moment avidly reading about the theater or acting in one amateur play after another. Unlike his father, his love was for acting rather than directing, and as he grew to manhood, though he decided upon a medical career, his interest in acting knew no diminution.

He had met Alice Gardner Plimpton while a medical student, and it was during his student days that they were married, sailing shortly afterward for Berlin, where young Peter was to take a post-graduate course at the University.

Ardently in love as he was, it was at first incomprehensible and somewhat of a disappointment to him that Alice—his charming, beautiful, capable Alice—had neither the ability nor the desire to act. At first he tried to kindle in her a love for acting, but he finally abandoned the effort. However, though she could not share her husband's penchant for acting, she loved the theater itself, appreciated his talent and encouraged it.

But that was Alice Cornell's way. She possessed that rare faculty of encouraging and stimulating others. There was in her a shining and abiding faith in life, in people, in the goodness of human nature. Physically, she was strikingly attractive. Her figure slenderly rounded, she was of medium height—five feet five inches—with an abundance of lustrous dark hair and warm hazel eyes which gazed trustfully out upon what was to her a singularly beautiful world. She carried her smartly coiffed head with an air of breeding and distinction. Upon meeting her one was instantly impressed with a sense of warmth, vitality, friendliness. People had a way of bringing their troubles to her and asking her advice about things. No matter where she was, in Buffalo or Berlin, she had a knack of making and keeping friends.

Upon completion of Peter's post-graduate course in the German capital, the Cornells returned to Buffalo where Doctor Cornell established his practice. With them was their six-months-old daughter, Katharine, who had been born in a Berlin pension—on February 16, 1898. Gazing at the child, people remarked that it was a fine, healthy youngster with a lusty and *carrying* voice. Alice would look across at Peter and they would smile a little proudly at each other, for only they knew how frail the mite had been at birth and how for months they had had to battle to sustain life in that tiny body, which had weighed not quite three pounds. They remembered the first few months of her life when, as was then the German practice, they kept her lying on a board, wrapped in cotton batting. There had been dreadful days when Peter Cornell, just twenty-seven years old, had walked the tidy streets of Berlin trying to prepare himself for the death of his only child. She cried so much that the Cornells were usually asked to leave the places where they stayed, but gradually the little cheeks began to fill out in endearing baby roundness, gradually her weight had increased, and they knew at last that their daughter would live.

Back in Buffalo, despite his substantial practice, Peter Cornell plunged into amateur theatricals again, and so it was that almost the first words which formed the child's vocabulary were "play," "show," "part," "costume," "make-up," "cue"—words which belonged to the magical, other-world called *Theater*. Sensitive, restless, impressionable, she began even in kindergarten producing plays of her own. It was fun—it was more fun than hopscotch or blind man's bluff or farmer-takes-a-wife.

The day she started for kindergarten was a memorable day in Kit's life. She came down to breakfast looking very spic and span, and her father, who was always the personification of neatness, glanced at her approvingly. To Kit, like any other little girl, entering kindergarten was an event. She faced it with both eagerness and trepidation. Her eggs being served, she began to eat them nervously, her mind not on the food, but on what lay ahead. Then came the accident. She spilled some egg on her nice, clean dress. Guiltily, apprehensively, she looked at her father, hoping that he had not seen; but his eyes were regarding her sternly.

"When you come home from school," he told her, "you must practice for one solid hour—*how to eat eggs!*"

CHAPTER TWO

THE DOCTOR TURNS SHOWMAN

*K*INDERGARTEN CHANGED to school, and the play-giving continued. Plays were more fun than ever now, for the school had its auditorium and here plays and pageants were frequently put on, always gala occasions to which one's friends and parents were invited.

These exciting events were preceded by weeks of preparation, evenings after dinner reciting one's lines to Father or Aunt Lydia or Uncle Douglas, while Mother became very busy cutting out paper wings or crowns and making long, beautiful robes out of cheesecloth which somehow turned into celestial garments when, being an angel, one wore them in a pageant.

Mother was always very encouraging. Tenderly, while these preparations were going on, she would assure Kit that everything was going to be all right. Despite the fact that she was a doctor's wife, Mother had her own theories about many things. Temper, for instance. Mother always told Kit that when a person got angry, it was not because that person had a bad disposition. Oh, not at all! It was simply due to bad circulation. So on the rare occasions when the child lost her temper, Mother did not scold or punish.

12

She sent Kit out to run around the block. Kit never thought of disobeying this order. She ran around the block, never stopping, as fast as her skinny little legs could carry her. It was odd how well Mother's theory worked, for Kit always returned home, her face flushed, her eyes bright, and all anger happily dissolved.

It was lovely, being an angel in the pageants, although Mother would laugh—that ready, ripply laugh of hers—and say that her daughter did not look in the least like an angel and certainly did not *always* behave like one.

Kit was a restless, active, timid child, with a remarkable memory, and forever asking questions. Everything interested her (except perhaps elephants and arithmetic), and everything interested her *strenuously*. Halfheartedness was simply no part of her nature. Her love, though given warily, was given wholly; while if she disliked anyone, it distressed her even to be around them. Even as a child, she was intensely loyal.

Mother said that she was moody. The truth was that Katharine was an unhappy child. Sometimes this unhappiness was only vague and dull; sometimes it was sharp and tyrannical. She lacked the aggressiveness and shrewdness to cope with other children. She used to take piano lessons at the home of a school friend. One day, after the two children had practiced exceptionally well, her friend's mother gave them twenty cents for two ice cream sodas at Smither and Thurston's Drugstore on the corner. But on arriving at the drugstore, her friend met another friend.

"Hello."

"Hello. Where you going?"

"My mother gave me twenty cents for ice cream sodas.

Do you want one? Come on, I'll treat you to an ice cream
soda!"

Kit, not saying anything, stood there holding her bike,
shocked and hurt at her friend's perfidy. Even when the
two girls entered the drugstore, arms about each other,
leaving her outside, she was still speechless, too hurt to
speak. At last she got on her bike and started for home.
She had gone only a little way when she got off the bike
and stood there, crying very softly. She never told anyone
about that, not even Mother. But this shyness, this inability
to cope with children of her own age, brought her almost
incessant misery.

Too, she who loved beauty so keenly, felt always that she
was ugly. Acutely sensitive, she had few playmates and
avoided, rather than sought, friends of her own age. This
was a secret unhappiness, a strange self-dissatisfaction,
which she could not explain, could not talk about to anyone.

Externally, it was a childhood singularly blessed. There
was no lack of the niceties of living in the Cornell home,
there were no financial worries, there was no friction. Her
world, indeed, was a very gracious place. There were books
in it, beautiful books, although she loved the out-of-doors
too much to read many of them. There were all the toys a
child could want. There were trees which she learned to
climb with the agility and fearlessness of any boy in the
neighborhood. There was roller skating—whizzing down a
hill at breakneck speed, whirling around corners, and often
skinning a knee.

When Christmas came she could not understand why
it was that every other child in the world had a Christmas
tree, while she never had one. Wistfully, longingly, she

would walk along the street, gazing in the windows of the houses at tall, beautiful trees resplendently bedecked with candles and silver stars and varicolored globes and popcorn strung on a thread. Often she would say to herself, "Perhaps next year I'll have a tree, too!" but somehow, it never came. The family always gave her many presents and even pinned a stocking to the arm of the sofa in her mother's upstairs sitting room, but they never trimmed a tree for her. A Christmas tree was gorgeous and exciting. It never seemed quite like Christmas without one. Why wouldn't they give her a Christmas tree? She never knew the answer to the question.

But if there were no Christmas trees, there were always—always the plays. To Kit, the most fascinating thing in the world was being permitted to attend the grown-up rehearsals. Grandfather said she might come if she would keep very, very still. How, she wondered, could one do anything else at rehearsal? Just to sit, to watch, to listen—that was enough. She would hunch herself ungracefully on the stairs, her thin legs clasped at the knees, her dark, luminous eyes fixed steadfastly upon that most amazing place where most amazing things happened—the stage! There for hours quite motionless she would remain, eyes fastened upon Grandfather or Father or Aunt Lydia who suddenly, as if some magic wand had been waved over them, would become quite different persons from those they were at home.

She was a tall, thin, leggy child. There was something already old about that dark, pale, intense little face; something old and wise in the dark, widely spaced eyes. Not even those who loved her most called her a "pretty" child

in those days when "prettiness" was the vogue. The width
through the cheekbones gave a Slavic quality to her face,
and at that time when "rosebud" mouths were considered
the epitome of beauty, her mouth was too large. Her
straight, short hair was so dark a brown as to appear almost
black. Mother always parted it neatly in the center and
drew it back from the brows with a small, flat bow on each
side.

Summers the Cornell family spent at Grandfather Cornell's house in Coburg, Ontario. On very warm days Kit
was permitted to go swimming in Lake Ontario, a form of
sport at which she early became proficient. Too, on Grandfather's estate there were herds of cows, wide fields of vegetables, tall old trees and spacious gardens. It was fun to
help the cowmen at their tasks, to gather all the flowers
she wanted, to help pick the vegetables. There was a smooth
lawn, so smooth that it seemed almost like green marble.
There was a tennis court and two or three riding horses.
She rode horseback as soon as she was old enough, and
while still a child she drove her Grandfather's horse, named
Rubber because of his color. But most important of all at
the house in Coburg was the long gallery at the back. Here
in the gallery plays were put on, and when the place was
not in use by the older folk, Kit and her young neighbor,
Jo Pierce, would take charge of it, putting on their own
plays, plays which they themselves had written, all about
Queens and Dukes and Princesses.

When the collaborators considered that their play had
been sufficiently rehearsed, they gave their performance,
charging pennies for admission. Sometimes they made as
much as twenty cents, which did not always cover the cost

of production, but then, who cared about profits? Th thing
was to act—and to act beautifully.

Kit was eight when one day she went in searchf her
mother to tell her all about the new play she and had
written called, "The Hidden Treasure," in which intended to play the part of the Duke. She saw her her
first. He was a well-groomed man, slightly under m m
height and stockily built. Even now, at thirty-five, h as
beginning to grow bald, and the receding hairline e
his naturally rubicund face seem even rounder. Seate
posite him was her mother. Evidently she had just ret
from making afternoon calls, for she still wore her
a large, particularly becoming straw trimmed with flo
Her summer dress was of white muslin modishly
necked and long sleeved, its full, sweeping skirt edged
a narrow ruffle. Kit always thought her mother extren
beautiful, and certainly, Alice Cornell made a fetch
picture that day as she sat, holding her lace parasol w
its long slender handle, and watching her husband w
eyes that were fond and earnest.

"It seems odd," Kit heard her say as she approached
"that there won't ever be any more patients."

This, to the child, was a startling announcement. Father?
Without patients? She walked toward her mother and
leaned affectionately against her, the somber, unchildish
eyes questioningly upon her father. Alice's arm reached out
and tenderly encircled her daughter's waist.

"But of course," went on Alice brightly, "if that's what
you want to do, Peter—"

It was 1906, and little girls were taught to be seen and
not heard, so Kit said nothing. But even to one of eight

it was evident that Father was about to do something daring and momentous.

It was a time of national prosperity, a time of change. The horse was already giving way to the automobile, which was now no longer called a "horseless carriage," and which was no longer some strange contrivance at which people laughed and stared, and young boys called derisively, "Get a horse"! Automobiles were beginning to be considered quite safe, and ladies, "going automobiling" were suitably attired with a long natural linen coat called a "duster," goggles, and a voluminous veil tied about the hat and under the chin. "In the Shade of the Old Apple Tree" and "Wait Till the Sun Shines, Nellie," were the popular tunes being sung about parlor pianos. Here and there a new form of entertainment called the "Nickelodeon" was emerging. These were the first motion-picture houses—small, badly aired places, to which no refined person ever went. It was the consensus of opinion that these new moving pictures would not last, that they were merely a fad, and that, anyhow, they would never have any appeal except for the lower classes.

An actor felt that it amounted to absolute disgrace to play in a moving picture. He had only one excuse for doing so, and that was that he was penniless. Theatrical business itself was in its heyday. "Road shows" were going out from New York and Chicago by the hundreds, many of them to be stranded in faraway places. As yet actors had no union, no way of protecting themselves against such a catastrophe. Every theater curtain had its "peephole," and before each performance actors would cluster about the peephole to see the size of the house, for whether or not they got their salaries at the end of the week often depended upon the number of what they called "customers" who came to see the show.

In those days an actor's life was one of incessant wandering. Theatrical companies came to Buffalo, sometimes playing a week at The Star, and then went on—east, west, north, south—tours which in theatrical parlance were always referred to simply as "the road." And now, as her parents continued their discussion, it developed that Peter Cornell was giving up his profession to become part-owner and manager of The Star!

Father, managing a real theater! It was glorious and exciting. Having a father who was associated with a real theater somehow set one apart from the rest of the mundane world.

"Why, Kit," Mother suddenly said, "you've got ink on your new dress! Darling, why won't you be careful?"

Ink! Dress! As if anything mattered! Eyes aglow with pride in him, Kit gazed up at her father. He was smiling, gazing out into space over her head as if he, too, were suddenly above such everyday things as ink and clothes. For him there would be no more counting pulses, no more listening through stethoscopes and looking at tongues, no more prescriptions to write, no more patients sitting fearfully in the huge leather chair facing his desk. He was about to become part of a world which had held him always under a singular enchantment. Already he was planning innovations for The Star, changes in personnel, changes in the lobby display.

Dr. Peter Cornell could not look ahead. He could not foresee how much this change was to affect the future of his daughter. Something more than mere personal desire was at work in shaping his decision, something unrecognized and unknown, yet working surely, working invisibly, but leading onward and upward to a splendid and shimmering goal.

The Cornells had outlined no career for Katharine. If someone had told them that summer afternoon in 1906 that this dark, moody, imaginative child would one day be acknowledged as "The First Lady of the American Stage," they would have looked at each other and gasped. They wanted their daughter to grow up into a useful, healthy, happy woman, they visualized for her no greater glory than this. They planned to give her the best education they could afford, and already Peter Cornell had begun to instill into that quick, receptive and retentive mind the principles of discipline, of resourcefulness, of perseverance, of reliability, of consideration for others—traits of character which were later to stand her in good stead, for experiences vast and portentous awaited her.

CHAPTER THREE

KIT MAKES UP HER MIND

$\mathcal{B}$UT ONE grows accustomed to anything, even to the fact that one's father is the manager of a real theater. And to Kit that which at first seemed incomprehensible became, after a time, merely a matter of course. Kit was not yet old enough to be taken to see the plays; besides, there was school and an ever-increasing amount of homework to do, and there was a developing interest in athletics.

For a long time now she had had a punching bag and trapeze in her nursery, and she became so expert on the trapeze that she was asked to perform as a gymnast at a charity circus. Among the other acts was a professional acrobat who did a hobo act on a slack wire. Watching him spellbound, it came to her that perhaps the most wonderful thing a person could do in this humdrum world was to be able to walk on a slack wire. Here was ambition, indeed. She fancied herself a glorified being of incredible lightness, walking the wire with a kind of divine nonchalance, and even dancing upon it with a gaily colored parasol in one hand. A bit shyly, she discussed it later with the acrobat, who seemed to agree with her that it was a worthy goal. In fact, he made her a present of his slack wire. She could scarcely wait to put it up, and the next day, taking no one

into her confidence, she did so. Now she must teach herself
to walk it. Her father did not know she had the slack wire,
and discretion being always the better part of valor, she did
her practicing when he was not at home. The slack wire
became her most cherished possession. This, indeed, was
thrilling—she, of all the kids in Buffalo, had a slack wire!

With characteristic zeal, young Kit, aged ten, took up
the art of wire walking, practicing so conscientiously that
in a comparatively short time she could sustain herself
upon the wire with a certain amount of ease. Promptly she
was the envy of every child in the neighborhood. The ambition among the younger set to become slack-wire walkers
became something of an epidemic. Suddenly Kit found
herself popular, even courted. She was even known to accept bribes of candy and ice cream cones for the privilege
of walking on her wire. Boys and girls swarmed into the
Cornell back yard and took their tumbles with resignation.
If you fell and got a bump on your head, it was all in a
worthy cause. The only thing to do in such case was to
climb grimly back on the wire determined that this time you
would stay up. What might have been a brilliant career in
the delightful art of wire walking ended abruptly when Kit
sprained her ankle, and her father dismantled the apparatus
as a precautionary measure.

Kit bore this philosophically because her ankle had to be
done up in a splint and, like all children, she enjoyed wearing splints and bandages. Shortly after the splint was removed, she made the discovery that the foyer of the theater
was almost as good a place to roller skate as a rink. It was
wide and smooth and it sloped a little. Oldsters in Buffalo

can still recall standing in line at the box office and watching a dark-eyed child careening about them on roller skates. There is reliable authority for the story (although later Kit would never vouch for it) that she once rode a *horse* through the lobby. Substantiation of this, however, states that the stable from which the horse was hired was *Twothy's.*

But on the whole a theater lobby is better as a rink than as a bridle path. Now and then Kit would halt in her skating to stand gazing at the posters, those ever-changing, ever-fascinating posters in the lobby.

Maxine Elliott, statuesque and incredibly beautiful. Julia Marlowe, who always looked so sad. Sarah Bernhardt, whose hair always looked untidy. Nazimova, exotic and exciting. Tiny Marie Doro, so lovely it was difficult to believe that she was constructed of mere human flesh like ordinary mortals. Actresses all seemed possessed of one common attribute—beauty. Gazing at the posters, it seemed impossible to believe that these actresses had ever climbed trees or been kept in after school. The idea persisted that one *had* to be beautiful to be on the stage.

The idea that she would ever be an actress had not yet occurred to Katharine Cornell. When she thought about her future at all, she thought it would be rather nice to be a trained nurse. Then one day posted in front of The Star were bills which read:

"COMING
MAUDE ADAMS
in
PETER PAN"

This was an event, not only to the Cornells, but to the entire city of Buffalo. "Peter Pan" had been first produced in America at the Empire Theater in New York City in 1905. It had made one of the greatest hits in the history of the theater. After a satisfactory run, it had been sent, as plays usually were in those days, "on the road." All America had heard of Maude Adams in "Peter Pan." Every theater manager in the country was clamoring to book the star and the play. Maude Adams in "Peter Pan" meant packed houses.

Kit had heard about "Peter Pan," and she raced, lickety-split, home to her mother, bursting into the house with the question: "May I go? May I go see 'Peter Pan'?"

Mother smiled indulgently. "Why, of course, dear. I wouldn't have you miss it for the world. We'll go to the Saturday matinee."

Waiting was torture; but finally came the very morning of the day.

Mother kept saying: "Now, dear, you *must* eat your breakfast."

Kit was too excited to think about food. Anticipation had grown so acute that it was like an ache, and now that it was no longer a question of days but only a question of hours, the hands of the clock seemed suddenly paralyzed.

Finally, she was walking to the theater with Mother, but it was difficult to walk. She had to restrain herself to keep from running.

"There's no hurry," Mother told her. "We've plenty of time."

Urgency seemed imperative. Yet, when at last they walked down the aisle and into the stage box, Kit closed her eyes, suddenly afraid it would be *too* beautiful. She heard the orchestra tuning up, then heard them playing. But it was all confused, like a dream. In her impatience it was agony to sit still. She began to squirm restively as the lights were dimming, and Mother whispered: "Ssh! *Curtain going up!*"

Curtain going up. Three words. Suddenly they took on wondrous significance. In that moment they created in Katharine Cornell a feeling of awe, of momentous experiences impending.

As the entrance of Maude Adams became more and more imminent, Kit's excitement mounted to such a pitch that she left the box and hid herself in the heavy velvet drape which enclosed it. Gradually, as she heard Maude Adams speak, she was able to look at the stage, and finally to return to her seat in the box.

For the next three hours she existed in a world of enchantment. For days afterward the singular spell lingered. Wendy. The Never-never boys. The answering cry of "*Yes!*" from the audience when, as Tinker Bell is dying, Peter, with outstretched arms, rushes down to the footlights asking in a ringing voice: "*Do you believe in fairies?*"

Kit was ten and she was rapidly outgrowing all belief in fairies, yet from that day it seemed that a fairy wand had indeed been waved over her. Suddenly she was grown up. Suddenly she knew exactly what she wanted to do, what she wanted to be. She had arrived at this decision without any conscious thought. Quite abruptly everything was settled, everything was fixed.

She was going to be an actress!

No longer did it seem proper to skate in the lobby of the

theater. Now she walked into it sedately and gazed up at the posters with new eyes. What if, one day, she should see her own picture in one of those frames?

Leaving the lobby she would look up at the marquee with its many lights. She could even imagine her own name outlined in the glittering electric bulbs. One day, perhaps, on the posters outside would be the words:

KATHARINE CORNELL
in ......

For a time she kept this dream very secret, hugging it tenaciously within herself, afraid to speak of it, even to Mother, even to Grandmother. It would happen. She did not know when, she did not know how, but someday she was going on the stage. It was as inevitable as Christmas.

She thought of it all the time. She thought of it even when she went walking with Grandmother Plimpton, whom she loved with great affection. To Kit, Grandmother Plimpton was one of the most wonderful women in the world.

. Grandmother could tell endless stories about cities all over the world, about Kit's uncles and aunts, and especially about Grandmother's own brother, Kit's great-uncle Harry, who was burned to death in the Volunteer Fire Service of Buffalo. Grandmother could not walk very well or very far because she had rheumatism, and walking with her, Kit always limped too, asking over and over, "Does it hurt very much?"

As days passed she became too filled with this glorious new idea, too charged with it to remain silent, and one day she told Mother about it. This was no childish plea for encouragement. It was the calm, dignified announcement of a fact.

"I'm going on the stage."

She had expected Mother to laugh, but Mother looked down at her with a long, quiet gaze and answered, "You might change your mind."

Kit knew that she would not. She knew it as surely as she knew she was living. Sometimes there would be misgivings, sharp and devastating. At night after she went to bed there were lengthy conversations when she seemed to be two selves—Katharine and Kit.

"You! You can't be an actress! Actresses have to be pretty. You're not pretty," scoffed Katharine.

"I don't care. I'm going on the stage just the same," replied Kit recklessly.

"You've got a funny mouth and your eyes are too far apart," insisted Katharine.

"I don't *care!*"

"Father says actors and actresses have a dreadful time."

"I don't care about that, either. I don't care *how* hard it is. I don't care if I starve!"

"How do people *get* to be actresses, anyhow?"

"I don't know. There'll be a way. There's got to be."

"Huh! A fine actress you'll make! You, with your plain face!"

"I *will* be an actress! I will!"

Eleven years old. Twelve. The dream persisted. The theater drew her like a magnet. She loved it, loved every part of it, everything about it. The lobby. The auditorium. The dressing rooms. Even the smell, that indescribable backstage odor peculiar to old theaters. That lovely hush which descends upon the audience the moment before the curtain goes up. She read everything she could find about plays and players.

Almost every town in America had its stock company which, with the same cast, produced a new play each week. Particularly in summer did the stock companies flourish. Admittedly one of the best of these was the Jessie Bonstelle Company which came to Buffalo and played at The Star each summer. All Broadway managers spoke respectfully of Jessie Bonstelle and her organization, often entrusting her to "try out" many of their plays before they were put into rehearsal preparatory to New York openings.

Stock companies were that branch of theatricals in which the actor worked hardest. Invariably rehearsals were called for ten o'clock every morning, for while playing one play at night the actors had to rehearse a new play during the day. The Jessie Bonstelle Stock Company was no exception.

Jessie Bonstelle, even in her late thirties, was an energetic, dynamic, friendly person. Of medium height, always smartly dressed, with a wealth of reddish-blond hair and a face remarkable for intelligence rather than beauty, she was a capable executive. She engaged her own company, chose her own plays, directed rehearsals and played the leading feminine roles—a feat which required not only stamina but a prodigious capacity for work.

"What's your name, little girl?" she asked one morning of the earnest-faced youngster who seemed always standing around the theater, eying her with something curiously akin to awe.

"Katharine," answered the child shyly, "but people call me Kit."

"Kit what?"

"Kit Cornell."

"Oh. You're Doc' Cornell's daughter?"

"Yes."

"How old are you?"

"I'm twelve going on thirteen." There was a question Kit had been wanting to ask for a long time, and now she summoned up courage to ask it, speaking quickly, even a bit breathlessly. "Please, I—is it all right if I—would you mind if—may I—oh, please could I watch the rehearsals?"

"Why, of course you can, my dear. Any time."

"Oh, thank you! I—I'll sit 'way in the back row and you won't even know I'm there!"

Amused at the child's intensity, Miss Bonstelle smiled. "Why do you want to watch rehearsals? Heavens, I should think a child your age would rather be out playing games!"

"Oh, no! You see, I—I—" fearful of being hurt, Kit broke off confusedly, blushed, looked down at the ground in an agony of self-consciousness.

Suppose Miss Bonstelle, who knew so much about show business, should say she couldn't be an actress because her shoulders were too wide or because her left ankle turned in a little or because she was not pretty enough?

"You want to go on the stage yourself, someday, is that it?" asked Miss Bonstelle.

"Yes," Kit admitted.

But Miss Bonstelle did not laugh. She gave Kit a slight, reassuring pat on the shoulder. "Well," she answered, "hurry and grow up and perhaps you can play Jo for me."

Even now Miss Bonstelle saw in her the very child that Jo must have been. Jo in "Little Women" was Kit's favor-

ite character, but she walked away from the theater thinking
that surely Miss Bonstelle had not meant that. The important thing at the moment, however, was that she had received Miss Bonstelle's permission to watch rehearsals—
any time.

Any time to Kit meant as soon as possible after school
was out. School was St. Margaret's Episcopal School, and
it was out at one-thirty. Day after day she would sit in the
darkened theater, a lonely, silent figure, absorbing watching, learning.

Though the plays were varied, rehearsals followed an
identical pattern. On the stage the lights would be turned
on. In the middle of the stage and as close to the footlights
as possible, a bare wooden table and a kitchen chair were
placed. Here sat the stage manager. The stage manager is
not the director. When the play is in progress, it is his
business to see that the sets are correct, that props are
ready, to produce off-stage noises, to give the signal for the
fall of the curtain; while at rehearsals he lays out the scenes
and follows the manuscript, prompting the actors when
they falter in a line. When the company assembled for
rehearsal, they found merely a bare stage, and the stage
manager marked out the set, using stage braces for this
purpose.

Stage braces are two narrow slabs of wood joined together, which can be shortened or elongated by turning
a screw in the center. Their real purpose is to brace the
scenery. One end has an iron hook, while the other end
has iron holes through which screws are put into the floor
of the stage. The stage manager would take these long
pieces of wood, laying them upon the floor. Sometimes he

would place them end to end, at other times he would leave a space between, announcing as he did so, "This is the window," "This is the entrance to the garden," "This is the door into the drawing room."

The company listened closely to this, their eyes earnestly upon him. Then he would take some straight-backed chairs and place them about the stage, saying, "This is the piano," "This is the divan," or "This is the bed," or "This is the tree." Having explained it all, he would seat himself at the table, glance down at the manuscript, and call out pleasantly, "All right, folks. Act one!"

Actors received their next week's parts on Tuesday mornings. The parts were limp little books of typewritten pages with pale blue covers. An actor meticulously wrote upon them in pencil every direction his director gave him. If Miss Bonstelle said, "On this speech, Harry, cross left," the actor penciled "X L" opposite the line in his part.

It did not take the child in the back row long to familiarize herself with the curious jargon which belongs to the actor alone. For instance, the part above the stage is called the "flies." Footlights are alluded to simply as "the foots." A small spotlight is "a baby spot." A player saying, "Business with cup" meant that he was announcing to himself and to Miss Bonstelle, the directress, that he remembered that at this point he was supposed to have some action in which a cup was involved. The cup itself, or anything handled by the actors during the action of the play, was called a "prop." The actor's actions were always referred to as "business." "Business of opening letter," an actor would say, when there was no letter in his hand at all.

Sometimes one of the players would stop in his speech

and cry nervously, "Throw me the line!" One might rea-
sonably expect the stage manager to toss out a rope, but
instead he merely read the speech from the manuscript, to
which the actor would say, "Oh, yes,"—and continue playing his part.

When an actor declared, "I went up last night," or "I
was up higher than a kite," he did not mean that he took
a trip in an airplane, he meant that he forgot his lines.
While if one said, "I broke him up," he meant that on the
stage he made some foolish error which caused his fellow
player to so far forget himself as to laugh when such a
laugh was not required in the scene. The expression, "I'm
up in that part" meant that the actor knew the lines of the
part. "Up stage" meant the back of the stage. "Down
stage" meant close to the footlights. Yet when an actor
referred to another as putting on airs, he would say scath-
ingly, "Oh, he's terribly upstage!"

To the wide-eyed child watching all this, it was like a
new world opening before her. Hungrily, she absorbed it.
She learned that an actor resents nothing so much as
being forced by another actor to play "upstage" to him,
meaning that his fellow player, by taking a position above
him on the stage, forces him to play his scenes with his
back halfway to the audience.

She learned that an actor possessed the knack of trans-
forming himself in an instant into an old man, a drunkard,
a cripple, a King or a beggar. Often Miss Bonstelle would
stop in her speech and looking at the stage manager, ask,
"Is this where I cross?"—and she would be simply Miss
Bonstelle asking a question. Eyes still on the manuscript,
the stage manager would nod, and Miss Bonstelle would

walk across the stage. But the odd part of it was that she did not walk across the stage *as Miss Bonstelle;* in that instant, miraculously, she would not *be* Miss Bonstelle any longer. In that instant she would change and actually be the character she was playing, walking across the stage as that character would walk. It was as if an actor could shed his own personality even more readily than he could shed his overcoat.

Sitting there, little Katharine Cornell would clasp her thin hands tight and remind herself that someday *she* would be up there on the stage, rehearsing like that. Someday *she* would have a part to read. Someday an actor would be saying to *her,* "That's your cue!"

As Miss Bonstelle returned to Buffalo summer after summer during Kit's school years, she and Kit became friends. "Do you still want to be an actress?" she would ask laughingly.

"More than anything in the world!"

Then Miss Bonstelle would laugh and say, "All right. Hurry and grow up."

Kit was growing—and growing fast. She had always been a shy child, and as she reached her early teens this shyness, rather than diminishing, increased. She knew her own faults too well for her own comfort. There was this distressing shyness, for instance, this awful self-consciousness. How were they to be remedied?

Bleak and dreadful were moments when she stood alone in her room, gazing at herself in the mirror. In her acute self-depreciation, she saw herself distortedly, exaggerated her flaws. At thirteen she was tall for her age, awkward, but it is not conducive to poise and self-confidence to keep reminding oneself that one is too tall, too bony, too angular, that one's mouth is too big, one's feet too big, one's shoulders too wide. According to herself, everything was wrong with Katharine Cornell.

Looking at her impersonally, a stranger saw quite another person. True, he saw a tall, slender girl who had not yet learned grace; a girl with dark, straight hair neatly parted in the middle, with a long, heavy braid reaching to below her waist in the back, and caught at the nape with a wide bow of crisp taffeta ribbon. True, it was not a face of the vacuous "cuteness" then considered chic. But it was a face singularly intelligent, arresting, strong, expressive. The mouth, though wide, was beautifully shaped. The nose was perfect. The eyes—dark, clear, deeply set and widely spaced —were the eyes of a dreamer, a poet. They were not the eyes of a thirteen-year-old, they were the eyes of a woman. The face itself was not yet a mask for the deep emotions within. It was mobile, reflecting candidly every innermost thought. It was a face so clearly planed that a sculptor would have enjoyed reproducing it in clay. There was beauty in that young face, beauty which had nothing to do with the shape of brow or chin or cheek. Her body was lithe, muscular, healthy. She was a good scholar, if not an exceptionally brilliant one. She excelled in athletics, especially tennis and swimming.

It was impossible to foresee how the style of feminine beauty was to change during the coming years. Already the Gibson girl, queenly and statuesque, had been superseded by the fluffy, ultra-feminine type. Considered beautiful now, was someone small, dainty and be-curled, with a short nose and a tiny, puckery mouth, called "The Nell Brinkley

Girl." Comparing herself to this standard of beauty, of which she was the direct opposite, young Katharine Cornell saw herself as actually *homely*, and since she could not change her weight, the width of her shoulders, the size of her mouth, the shape of her face, she realized that there was simply nothing she could do about it, and she told herself that she would just go on being homely all the days of her life.

Even then, when most girls are awakening to the importance of clothes, Kit was not particularly interested in them. As far as was possible she avoided the lacy, festive type of garments then considered smart. She felt at home in middy blouses, low-heeled shoes, coats with deep, roomy pockets, sports clothes and crisply tailored frocks.

Mother, who usually understood people so well, could not understand why it was difficult for Kit to talk to strangers. Kit blamed herself for this and tried desperately to overcome it. For after all, an actress should be gay, should be charming, should be brilliant, should be at ease everywhere and with anyone, should be interested in everything and everybody.

Growing up had its compensations. At least, the shame of "Timmy Toodleshanks" had become part of the past. When she was very little, her father had had a leather placard on which "Timmy Toodleshanks" had been stamped in gold letters. When Kit cried, he hung this placard about her neck and to her childish mind it had been a veritable badge of shame. For a long time now the placard had not made an appearance, perhaps because if she did any crying these days, she did it in the privacy of her own room.

Finally, Kit was fifteen and her parents decided that it
was time she went away to boarding school. Later, they
hoped, there would be Bryn Mawr. St. Margaret's Episcopal
School, which she had been attending in Buffalo, was a
grammar school. Oaksmere was a preparatory school, the
equivalent of "high."

It was 1913, and Mother and her sister, Aunt Lucy, were
talking about the new hobble skirts which reached just
below the ankles and forced women to walk with a curious
mincing gait; about the largeness of the muffs that would
be carried that winter, flat muffs which covered the entire
lap; about the extraordinary width of the hat brims, hats
which made one look topheavy with their burdens of willow
plumes, flowers, aigrettes. While Father, commenting upon
the news in his evening paper, discussed the Balkan League
and its war against Turkey. It was his opinion that the
Balkan War was not going to stop with the Balkans.

"It will spread," he declared quietly. "You'll see. Unless
this thing is stopped, it will spread all over Europe. War's
like a virus. You've got to stop it before it goes too far."

Some of his friends agreed with him. They began to
discuss Germany and her growing power, her resources, her
vast strides in chemical research, the growth of her navy,
her increasing dominance in commerce.

"Germany," shouted the German Kaiser, "must expand!
Germans are the salt of the earth! Germany is clad in
shining armor!"

To which the German populace, intoxicated with self-
glorification, answered feelingly, *"Hoch der Kaiser!"*

The rest of the world was becoming a bit uneasy under
all this bombastic talk of "German superiority," "Germans,

the super-race," "German shining armor," "Germany's mailed fist." England, her hands full at the moment with civil war in Ireland, was watching Germany apprehensively.

All this left young Katharine Cornell quite unmoved. She was engrossed with the interesting business of growing up. Next year she would be sixteen, and when one is sixteen one becomes, miraculously, a young lady. Besides, she was going away to boarding school—the Oaksmere School in Mamaroneck, Long Island.

Mamaroneck, Kit kept reminding herself, was close to New York City, and New York was the theatrical center. Life to her would not be worth living unless it could be lived within the proximity of theaters and unless it held the hope of eventual success as an actress.

It was not her first trip to New York. She remembered how thrilled she had been when her father had taken her to the Hippodrome to see one of the great spectacles that were always being held there. She thought she must have been about ten then. Now, of course, she would be able to visit New York City often. She would do her shopping there and go to matinees as frequently as possible. It was all rather wonderful.

At fifteen there were moments of utter tragedy and desolation when the goal seemed as remote as heaven. But there were moments, too, when despite the fact that she was on the verge of being grown up, had a Peter Pan rushed at her with the sudden question: "Do you believe in fairies?" she still would have answered with intensely joyous conviction: "Yes!"

CHAPTER FOUR

FIRST STEPS TOWARD THE GOAL

*T*HE SUDDEN death of her mother in 1915, two years after she became a student at Oaksmere, brought Katharine Cornell her first real sorrow. For a year before she died, the family knew that Alice was not well. But her death, as the result of a heart attack, was sudden. The passing of Alice Cornell left in her daughter's life a void which was never really to be filled. To Kit, a world without Mother in it, without her sympathy and encouragement, her tenderness and love and laughter, seemed strange and empty. For a long time, even after Katharine had returned to school, it seemed impossible for her to adjust herself to the fact that her mother—warm, vital, scintillant—would not be there waiting to welcome her when she came home on vacations. Yet Alice Cornell was not dead; she lived—and she still lives, a lovely, ever-gracious figure—in her daughter's memory.

Kit was never the sort to make a show of grief or to dramatize it. Though she loved her mother more than anything in the world, that world remained with its claims upon her interest, its urgent activities, its drama, its beauty.

Oaksmere School believed in developing the individuality and the talents of its students. Until Kit went there, the school had no real dramatic organization. It was her interest in theatricals which awakened the interest of a small part of the student body, when it was revealed that she could not only design sets, act in plays and produce them, but she could even write them. The girls worked hard at their plays and their pantomimes, an activity in which the new pupil, one Katharine Cornell, was swiftly conceded to be their leader. Not for nothing had she attended the Bonstelle rehearsals.

Even in her mid-teens she had the faculty of clear, clean-cut, vivid visualization and the gift of imparting what she visualized to those about her. Mentally, she was expanding, growing. For the first time she began to appreciate the value of a healthy body, a body trained to respond to emotion. She found that she could express with her body as well as her face, her voice, her eyes. She began to respect her body, its suppleness, its obedience. Quietly she was studying, analyzing, searching, groping. Slowly she was coming to realize a power within herself, as yet latent, but nonetheless present—an ability to project her emotions to her audience. There continued to be those agonizing moments of doubt, intervals of abysmal depression when, alone, she fought for faith, faith to persevere and to accomplish.

Tennyson's line, "We have but faith, we cannot know . . ." echoed within her mind. She *must* have faith. She must fight for it, if need be. Faith in what? In herself. There were times when that faith came gloriously to blossom, when it shone out of her eyes and when it was reflected in the very way she walked and held herself, times when she felt uplifted, free, invincible.

But there was so much she lacked, so much she wanted to know, so much she longed to express. Everything connected

with the stage was fascinating. Avidly she read the lives of
great actors of the past. How tempestuous and how colorful
were those famous tragedians of other days, how they flew
into rages—William Macready, Salvini, Edwin Forrest,
Edmund Kean. Then in contradiction to these human
volcanoes there was Edwin Booth, the greatest actor of
them all, a mild, shy, gentle little man, always mindful lest
he hurt anyone's feelings. And there was the fabulous
Henry Irving, who died in 1905, a being of exquisite self-
control, modest, dignified, patient, unhurried. These were
the hallowed names that had made stage history, these
people had given art and dignity to the stage. There was
Garrick, a small man who stuttered slightly, who had been
the first to introduce footlights. In his day unless an actor
were fortunate enough to secure the patronage of some
powerful noble, he was legally branded as a rogue, a vaga-
bond, an outlaw, subject to arrest and imprisonment. In
the time of Queen Elizabeth when pilgrimages to America
were forming, actors were in such disrepute that no actor
was permitted to join the groups which ventured into the
new world. On the lists of early American settlers appear
men of every trade save that of acting. Thus, since players
were considered so low as to be debarred from making the
journey with respectable folk, America was for a long time
destitute of actors.

What a strange country it must have been, mused
Katharine, without any theaters, without a single actor in
the entire thirteen colonies! And what a difference nowadays, when the American theater was the most brilliant in
the world!

One of Kit's most treasured possessions was an auto-

graphed biography of the great Bernhardt herself, on which
was written, "À Katharine Cornell, avec sympathie, Sarah
Bernhardt." This book, which she prized so highly, was
stolen from her at boarding school.

Her favorite studies were psychology, the Bible, and the
history of the novel. She majored in psychology, in which
she was judged an excellent student. It was this study of
psychology which gave her an understanding of her associates which was later to be indispensable to her, gave her
an ability to deal with people and with situations.

Her father was interested, even pleased, when he heard
of his daughter's desire to go on the stage, but he shrugged
his shoulders and said lightly, "Oh, well, you know how
girls of that age are. Kit's just stagestruck. She'll get over it."

But Aunt Lucy Plimpton was worried. She wished she
could be sure that Kit *would* get over it. Amateur theatricals
were all very fine, but the stage as a profession was something quite different. She had heard that life on the stage
was wild and immoral. Actresses—well, of course, one must
be broadminded about everything, but—were actresses *quite*
ladies?

Returning to Buffalo during vacation, Kit met an actress
at a social occasion one evening. Middle-aged, growing
stout, Miss Rose Grover was the very essence of friendliness, and she gushingly invited Kit to call upon her next
day at the hotel.

"Oh," exclaimed the older woman effusively, "I'm so
glad to see you, Miss Cornell. So nice of you to come.
Didn't we have a lovely evening at the O'Neil's? Such
charming, hospitable people. Do sit down, dearie. Well,
now, tell me about yourself. You're still going to school?

How nice! And I suppose when you leave school you're going to get married and—"

"Oh, no!" answered Kit, "I'm going on the stage."

Miss Grover's entire demeanor changed. All warmth evaporated. She stared disapprovingly. "You want to go on the stage?" she asked sharply.

"I want very much to go on the stage."

"No! Don't be a fool. There are hundreds of girls, better looking than you are, girls more talented, girls with experience, girls who need money, tramping Broadway, getting nowhere! Why should you want to do that? You have everything you could possibly desire. Money. Social position. A home. Every one of those girls would give their heart's blood to change places with you. Take my advice. Stay here where you're well off."

"But you see, I—"

"I know. I know. You think that stage life is easy. It isn't easy," she broke in impatiently. "You're thinking of the glamour of the stage, you don't know how tawdry it can be, how terrible. I tell you, it's a heartbreaking game!"

"But it—"

"You don't know what you're talking about. You're only one of thousands of teen-age, silly, stagestruck girls. I beg you, for your own sake, get that idea out of your head. Find some nice boy and marry him—*that's* real, that's worthwhile. The stage—you don't know the hardships, the uncertainties, the bitter disappointments, the struggle, the competition. You don't know what it means to get old— to get old in show business! There's no greater tragedy in all the world!"

Hurt, bewildered, Kit sat staring at the woman who was now so visibly agitated.

"Forget it. Forget the stage," went on that suddenly bitter, strident voice. "Huh! Listen, have you any pull? Do you know any Broadway managers?"

"N-no, but—"

"You'll never succeed without pull. I mean it. Look at me! Twenty years of my life devoted to the stage. And what have I got to show for it? Oh, if I had my life to live over again! I tell you, you can't expect to get anywhere in show business without pull, these days! And suppose you do get a chance for a lead on Broadway? What have you got? Nothing. A year or two of prestige and your picture in the papers. Then what? Think of any number of actresses who were famous only a few years ago. Where are they now? What's become of them? Who knows? Who cares?"

Katharine picked up her gloves, her purse. This woman's bitterness could not touch her. She felt strong and free.

"Well, thank you. I'm sorry I—"

"I don't suppose I've stopped you," said Miss Grover in a dull, apathetic voice. "I don't suppose you'll take my advice. I might as well have saved my breath."

At the door Kit turned, a regal young figure, her head well up, her shoulders straight, her voice calm and triumphant.

"No," she answered composedly, "you can't stop me. Nothing can stop me—nothing. Oh, perhaps I shall never be a great actress, but I simply feel that I—must act. And nothing's going to stop me!"

She returned to school, her faith firm, her vision unwavering. Her words had been a challenge—to life, to fate, to whatever gods there be. It was more than words she had spoken that late summer afternoon. It was a solemn dedication.

Through reading and observation, she had learned that the stage would undoubtedly exact sacrifices, unceasing sacrifices. She faced that fact honestly, unflinchingly, though as yet she could not foretell what those sacrifices might be.

An actress, working in the theater during the evenings, cannot make "dates" like other girls. Her profession demands of her that she sacrifice to a large extent the joys of a home. It is impossible for the actress to make definite plans in her private life. She must be available for "the road," and when out of a job she must be more or less on call. Meals and all the normal routine of ordinary life become irregular for the actress. Too, if she has a headache or a cold or any of the usual disabilities, she cannot remain at home and pamper herself. If she finds herself inclined to put on weight, she must deny herself certain foods. Yes, the stage means many sacrifices.

Older people—grown worldly and cynical—are apt to scoff at the ardor and completeness with which youth surrenders itself to its chosen path in life. Seemingly impelled by some mysterious and mighty force beyond its own cognition toward the career of acting, music, singing, dancing, writing, architecture or painting, youth maintains a one-pointedness which in itself is closely akin to glory. Often so clear and clean and dynamic is the motivation that all else in the world save the achievement of this one goal seems unimportant, trivial, and even interfering, for here alone, here in obedience and service to this one talent, is the fulfillment and delight of the individual. And only by one's holding fast against all odds and obstacles to that sublime one-pointedness, that unshakable, unbeatable fixity of purpose, can one ultimately triumph. So now it was with young Katharine Cornell. To her, the calling of an actress was something high and fine. She would bring to it all her intelligence, all her verve, her energy, her aspiration. The stage to her was a kind of temple to which she could bring these priceless gifts gladly, unstintingly, as once young votaries had lain their garlands and their lives upon the altars of ancient Rome.

Never did she divulge the depth of her feeling to anyone. Her schoolmates declared that one of the most pronounced of Katharine Cornell's traits was her sense of humor. She could laugh at anything, even herself. The only things which she did not take lightly were those which had any relation to the stage. Her ability to produce plays was equaled only by her ability in athletics, and she saw that the fair play and good sportsmanship demanded upon the athletic field had their place also in the theater.

The play activities at Oaksmere increased as time went on and interest in them mounted. When it was announced that Theresa Helburn was coming to coach "Twelfth Night," excitement ran high. Kit was to play Malvolio. On the eve of the production the girl who was to play Sir Toby sprained her ankle at basketball. For a time everything was dark, and then Miss Helburn, late of Bryn Mawr, in true trouper spirit, jumped in and played Sir Toby herself. This production over, it was decided to put on another play called "Play," written by Katharine Cornell. To direct this,

Miss Helburn was instrumental in bringing Edward Goodman of the Washington Square Players to Oaksmere.

Edward Goodman of the Washington Square Players
coming to Oaksmere! Now, indeed, the zeal of the student
body knew no bounds. Expectation reached fever pitch, for
Edward Goodman had already received the respect of
Broadway.

All theater-minded New York was watching the progress
of the incredible Washington Square Players who, curiously
enough, had never played in Washington Square. The
organization first materialized in 1914-15. Living in the
vicinity of picturesque Washington Square was a group of
ambitious, impecunious young people vitally interested in
the stage. Though their theatrical experience was scarcely
less meager than their funds, they were rich in ideas, and
these robust youngsters decided that they would hire a
theater and put on their own plays. They would paint their
own scenery, make their own costumes, write their own
material, direct it, act in it. Though only a few of them
had so far risen above the rank of tyros, they had high
hopes and high courage. One thing united them—love for
the theater. They managed to raise enough money to rent
a small theater, the Bandbox, on East 57th Street, and
dauntlessly set to work, after naming themselves the Washington Square Players.

Their first director had been Edward Goodman. It was
planned that plays should be produced on Friday and
Saturday nights only. None of them knew whether they
would continue after the first few performances, for the
rental of the theater had absorbed almost every cent which
they had been able to raise. But they set about designing

their costumes, painting their scenery, staging their first program which consisted of three one-act plays and a pantomime.

There was no money for advertising and none of the workers received payment. They peddled seats among their friends at fifty cents apiece, and these friends filled the small, cheap theater on the opening night of February 19, 1915. But somehow, no one ever knew quite how it happened—hardboiled critics heard of the affair and came, prepared to laugh. They went away impressed. Here was freshness, here was originality.

Next day theater-conscious New Yorkers read glowing accounts of the Washington Square Players. And Saturday night, to the astonishment of the actors who had dolefully expected to play to empty seats, the theater was crowded. People came—and kept coming, kept watching. Demand for seats grew so insistent that presently the admission fee was raised to one dollar and instead of giving only two performances a week the organization was giving six. After a time they could even afford to pay small salaries to the leading players. It was not long before the tiny Bandbox Theater on 57th Street near Third Avenue became inadequate, and now they had taken the Comedy Theater near Broadway where now they were gaining prestige and prosperity even beyond their wildest dreams.

So it was this Eddie Goodman, a short, dark man with a mustache, who was now coming to Oaksmere to produce Kit's play.

He noticed the author—a tall, broad-shouldered, slim-hipped girl, who had an amazing capacity for work. Pretty? Well, no. She had something more than mere prettiness,

she had distinction. Talented? Decidedly. She would probably, thought Goodman, develop into a first-rate writer
someday. As an amateur actress she had faults, glaring
faults, but there was something about her—a singular magnetism, an emotional intensity. But, of course, she was
merely a subdeb amusing herself with acting while she
was in school, and he thought in time no doubt she would
go back to Buffalo or wherever it was she came from, and
settle down to a social life, evolving perhaps into either a
playwright or a novelist.

When the rehearsals were over, the performance given,
Goodman's work was finished, he came backstage to say
good-by. The Oaksmere students crowded about him,
thanking him for his helpfulness, begging him to come back
and put on more plays for them. Shy, gauche, the Cornell
girl stood apart from all this. He walked toward her, his
mind now occupied with the thought that he must not miss
the next train back to New York.

"Well, good-by, Miss Cornell. You gave a splendid performance."

"Good-by, Mr. Goodman, and thank you."

His dark eyes regarded her speculatively. "Did you ever
think of going on the stage?" he asked.

Think of it! When had she ever thought of anything else?
She stared at him and nodded, suddenly unable to speak.

"Well," he said, reading the intensity of her desire in
the glowing eyes, "if you decide to go on the stage, come
in and see me when you come to New York." And he
turned away, hurrying to catch his train.

She stood watching him go. Had Goodman given her an
invitation to Paradise, Katharine Cornell could not have

been more surprised. Almost all night she lay thinking about his brief, hurried words. Eddie Goodman, who certainly ought to know, had actually suggested that she go on the stage! More, he had even offered to help her. Why, what he had said practically amounted to a contract! It was too marvelous. She kept assuring herself that she had *not* been dreaming. "Come in and see me," he had said.

But, of course, she must first finish school. When school was finally finished, she returned to Oaksmere to coach plays. It was autumn, a year and a half after Goodman's chance remark, that she decided to go to New York and take a room there. It was unnecessary to ask financial assistance from anyone, for she had an income from her mother's estate. Her allowance was small and she would be obliged to be careful about expenditures.

Though in embarking upon a career in the theater she had encountered no parental opposition, such opposition would not have acted as a deterrent. Convinced that the stage was her *métier*, she would have gone straight ahead in spite of every opposing force.

She found a room in a boardinghouse run by a Miss Pennypacker on East 39th Street between Madison and Fifth Avenues. It was a top floor front room, large and sunny, in one of the dignified old "brownstone fronts." To chaperon Kit, Aunt Lucy Plimpton came to New York and took a room in the same boardinghouse.

The Washington Square Players had their business offices in the Comedy Theater. On arriving there next day, Kit found the offices crowded. Even long-established actors were now eager to be affiliated with this successful organization. Katharine Cornell waited, not knowing quite what to do. An hour. Two hours. Three. At length a door opened, Goodman rushed out, brushed past her, and was gone. Had he seen her? Did he remember her? What to do now? There was only one thing to do and that was to come back tomorrow.

But tomorrow followed the same pattern. She caught only a brief glimpse of Goodman, who this time gave her a negligent nod.

For days, for weeks, Katharine Cornell kept going back to the Comedy Theater. Apparently there was no hope of ever getting beyond the outer office.

Sometimes the office would be crowded; sometimes, especially on rainy days, it would be empty. Sometimes Goodman seemed not to know she was there, at other times he would call out, "Hello, how are you?" and be gone before she could answer.

The situation seemed hopeless. She could not force herself upon his notice. She did not know where else to go to look for work, and she realized that even had she known, her lack of experience would be an insurmountable barrier. Her only possible chance was here. Night after night she returned to her room, baffled, confused, fighting desperately against disappointment. Night after night she battled against a remorseless inner voice which tortured her with the argument that it was no use to go to the Comedy day after day; that she might as well give up and return to Buffalo; that Goodman, when he told her to come and see him, had been merely polite, that he had not meant it, that he had forgotten that he had said it.

It took fortitude to withstand these arguments. It took fortitude to go back to the Comedy Theater again and again. If only she had the courage to walk right up to him and say, "Look, I'm the girl from Oaksmere, remember me? Remember telling me to come and see you? Well, here I am!"—but she never did.

Then one day he paused beside her. "I'm having some people read parts. If you'd like to try, come along."

It was as casual as that. She had dreamed of this, hoped for it, prayed for it, and now when opportunity came she felt woefully unprepared for it. As she followed him down into the theater, her knees began shaking, her hands trembled, her heart began a wild tattoo, seeming to be in every part of her body at once. It was as if someone had switched on a current of fear which ran through her entire being, filling every cell, every nerve, every drop of blood with turmoil.

On the stage, people stood about in little groups. Some of them were laughing, chatting, smoking, as if reading a part were the most inconsequential thing in the world. How, she wondered, could they be so indifferent? No one spoke to her. Her feeling of *aloneness* was a ghastly thing. It was then she made up her mind that if she were ever in a company and she saw someone who knew nobody, she would speak to him. He need not, she told herself, speak back, but she at least could help him to feel easier.

Having seen the performances, she recognized Miss Florence Enright, who was one of the principal players. Miss Enright, she thought, looked very kind. Now and then Goodman would call out a name and someone would step forward, take the proffered part, and read it aloud. Katharine Cornell had the wild desire to run; to run away and never stop running. Body taut, hands icy, she waited, re-

minding herself grimly that people *did* live through these
things.

"Miss Cornell."

She found herself walking forward, reaching out for a
part, standing alone in the middle of the stage.

"All right, Miss Cornell," said Goodman. "Go ahead."

She began to read, stumbling over the simplest words,
realizing with dismay that something had happened to her
voice.

"Louder, Miss Cornell. Can't hear you."

She tried to speak louder, but her voice seemed suddenly
weak and unwieldy. She had the terrible thought that it
would be simpler to die. Some of the watchers were smiling
derisively. Quietly, pityingly, Goodman told her that she
would not do.

As she left the stage, Miss Enright spoke to her—something about not being discouraged. Blindly, Kit Cornell
hurried into the street.

Failure is a crushing thing. She kept walking in a fury of
self-condemnation, not caring where she went or what became of her. Would she ever get another chance? And if
she did would she face this same dreadful fiasco? What had
happened that her voice had disappeared? No one could
have heard a word she said. Well, she had failed. Might
as well admit it. She was no good.

After a time she realized that she was in front of Saint
Patrick's. Many had gone there, both Catholics and non-
Catholics, leaving Broadway behind, seeking courage
through the peace of the church. Katharine Cornell sank
into one of the back pews, and quietly, unrestrainedly, she

Ernest Bachrach

1. Katharine Cornell at home.

3. Katharine Cornell and her fath[er]

2. Alice Cornell and her
   daughter, Kathari[ne]

Vandamn

Vandamn

4. Katharine Cornell at the age of four.

5. Katharine Cornell at about fourteen.

6. As Jo in *Little Women* — 1919.

7. As Sydney Fairfield in *The Bill of Divorcement* — 1921.

8. Katharine Cornell in the garden of her Beekman Place home.

9. As Mary Fitton in *Will Shakespeare* — 1923.

10. As Iris March in *The Green Hat* — 1925.

11. As Ellen Olenska in *The Age of Innocence* — 1928.

12. Gertrude Macy lunching with a friend.

13. Guthrie McClintic.

14. Katharine Cornell and Brian **Aherne** in *The Barretts of Wimpole Street* — 1931-2.

15. Flush.

16. Guthrie McClintic and Katharine Cornell having tea in the garden of their Beekman Place home. Flush, the cocker spaniel, is shown with his mistress.

17. Katharine Cornell with Flush on vacation in Bermuda.

Gertrude Macy

18. Sneden's Landing, N. Y. — the week-end cottage of Katharine Cornell.

Vandamn

19. As Juliet — 1934-5.

20. Katharine Cornell at Sneden's Landing.

Vandamn

21. Rehearsing *St. Joan*. Reading from left to right — Eduardo Ciannelli, who **played** Peter Cauchon, Arthur Byron (Brother John Lamaitre), Katharine Cornell and Guthrie McClintic.

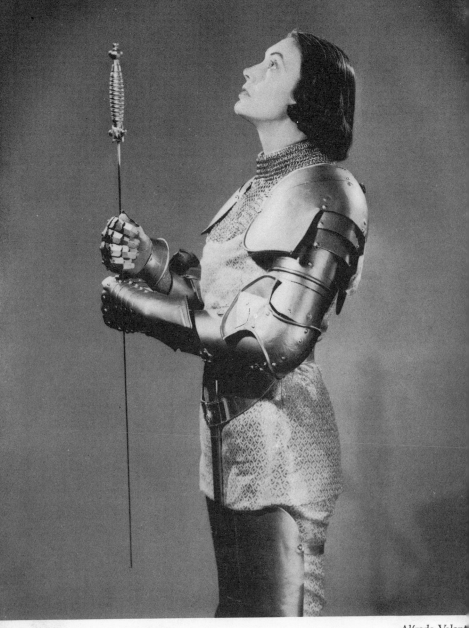

22. As Joan in *Saint Joan* — 1936.

23. As Oparre in *The Wingless Victory* — 1937.

24. On vacation in Garmisch, wearing a Bavarian dirndl.

25. A candid camera picture taken during a performance — 1940.

26. Alexander Woollcott visits Katharine Cornell backstage — 1941. Illo,
Miss Cornell's dog, shown with them.

27. Katharine Cornell in the drawing room of her New York home.

Vandamn

28. Katharine Cornell and Raymond Massey in *The Doctor's Dilemma* — 1941.

29. Katharine **Cornell** and Burgess Meredith in the last act of the all-star revival of *Candida* for the benefit of the Army-Navy Relief. Meredith was "on loan" from **the U. S. Army.**

Ernest Bachrach

30. As Rose Burke — 1942.

31. Scene from *The Three Sisters* — 1942-43. Left to Right —
Katharine Cornell, Gertrude Musgrove, Judith Anderson.

32. **Katharine** Cornell and Brian Aherne **giving a** radio performance of *The Barretts of Wimpole Street* for the benefit of the American Red Cross.

33. As Masha in *The Three Sisters*, taken backstage of the Ethel Barrymore Theatre.

34. Katharine Cornell in a scene from the film *Stage Door Canteen*
— 1943.

began to weep. Desperately, simply, as a frightened and bewildered child, she prayed.

"Oh, God, help me! *Please* help me! Tell me what to do!"

Presently she ceased praying and simply sat, staring wretchedly ahead for a long time.

"You've had your chance and you've failed," she told herself miserably.

At last she rose from the pew, all tears hidden now, and walked out into the sunlight, moving swiftly through the crowds of shoppers.

She would not give up. There must be a way and she must find it.

Finally she recalled the name of one of America's most well-known academies of dramatic art. She went there and interviewed one of the coaches. He was a suave, pleasant man, and his encouragement was heartening. Though flattered by his praise, some instinct prompted her to be wary. Perhaps, after all, he was only saying these nice things because he did not like to lose a prospective pupil. Besides, how did she know that she would find what she needed at this school?

"Well, I—before I decide definitely, I'd like to see one of your productions," she told him.

He seemed a trifle surprised at this, but he told her when the next production would be and invited her to come.

But when she had seen the production, she walked away telling herself that it was no better than those which had been done at Oaksmere. She knew that she would never go back to that school.

Seemingly she was up against a stone wall. What was she to do now? To whom could she turn for advice? She thought of her father, and decided to send for him.

When he came, he seemed not to think that this was so serious, after all.

"Well, don't you know anyone who can coach you?" he asked.

She remembered then the woman who had spoken to her at the Comedy Theater the day of her fiasco—Florence Enright.

CHAPTER FIVE

KIT'S CAREER BEGINS

"*F*LO" ENRIGHT was possessed of that rare and lovely thing—an understanding soul. She understood the courage that had motivated Katharine Cornell, forcing her to continued effort. She understood the humility which prompted her now, not to ask for another chance, but merely to ask for coaching so that when the next chance came she would be equipped to meet it. Miss Enright cheerfully took over the task of coaching, and at the end of a few weeks suggested that Kit attend rehearsals as an onlooker provided, of course, Eddie's permission could be secured.

"Sure," agreed Goodman, "let her come."

So day after day Katharine Cornell walked quietly, unobtrusively, into the theater, took a seat in the back of the house, and watched. She was never the sort to push herself forward, but in spite of her reticence it was inevitable that members of the organization should come to know her, to exchange greetings; even Goodman would stop in the aisle now and then. "Well," he would say genially, "how do you think it's coming along?" or, "Well, hello, Kit, didn't expect to see you today because of the storm. Terrible, isn't it?" No member of the cast was more prompt at rehearsals than the girl who had no part in them.

In the next bill they were to produce a one-act play, the action of which was laid in Japan, called "Bushido." The part of Shusai, a Japanese mother, was so small that the girl who was assigned to it did not even come to rehearsals, considering the part so insignificant that she did not need to rehearse it.

This was explained to Kit, and she was asked if she would read the part for the other girl. The part consisted of but four words: "My son! My son!"

Even though she knew that she was not going to play it at the performance, Kit walked along the street repeating those four words. She said them as she ate, as she bathed, as she lay in bed—"My son! My son!" For days she worked to achieve the glidelike walk of the Samuri woman, the right voice, the right make-up and coiffure.

One day when production was only a week off, she was told that she did not need to come the next day, as the girl who had been engaged for the part would be present to read it. That was the only rehearsal Kit missed. The next day when she came merely to watch, Helen Westley, one of the founders of the Washington Square Players, called her up to the stage.

"The girl doing Shusai didn't come," she explained.

Perhaps Kit's reading of those four short words was noticeably superior to that of the other girl, or perhaps because of the sustained thought which she had given to the character, this rehearsal was not like any that had preceded it, for when she had spoken those four words, rehearsal stopped, the actors broke out into spontaneous applause, and Goodman said: "Go see the wardrobe woman about your costume!"

This was the most exciting moment of Kit's life. She was at last actually a member of the Washington Square Players!

A few nights later Broadway saw Katharine Cornell for the first time. Broadway was not interested. Kit, however, was experiencing something akin to bliss. Insignificant though her part was, she was speaking a line in a real theater. It was a start in the right direction. It did not matter that there was no salary, since the Washington Square Players paid none except to their top actors.

The next rehearsals were for Andreyeff's "Life of Man." Again Katharine Cornell had a part, but this time Broadway heard rather than saw her, for all she had to do in the production was to scream off stage.

"Plots and Playwrights," a Harvard prize play which followed, brought her first real part, that of an artist. She played it creditably, but no Broadway manager came offering her contracts. Three people, however, gave her particular notice. One was the critic, Heywood Broun, who wrote of her that she was "a dead-white, young American Duse." Another was the press representative for William Farnum, Ray Henderson, who, as advance man, had often visited Buffalo and who already knew Doctor Cornell. Henderson wrote to Doctor Cornell that his daughter had "conducted herself like a professional." The third was a talent scout for the producer, Winthrop Ames, who, in the darkness of the theater, wrote himself a penciled note upon his program opposite the name of Katharine Cornell. He was a boyish-looking young man from Seattle named Guthrie McClintic, and his note to himself was: "Interesting—monotonous—watch."

Katharine Cornell's character had already molded. It was the same at eighteen as it is at forty-five. She was never prone to dream glorious, soaring dreams. She had no burning desire to play Juliet or any special part. She was merely "walking along a road" which she *must* travel.

Never did she try to force things. She was nervous, deeply sensitive, intelligent, restless, often changeable. Her mind was quick and responsive. Over even the smallest detail, she was an exact and painstaking worker.

She was ardently receptive to direction and to every opportunity for growth and development. Her memory was excellent, although she remembered faces better than she remembered names. Had she not been an actress, she would probably have devoted herself to music. Music, especially symphonies, held her enthralled. She felt at times a definite *need* for music, as people feel the need for food.

In spite of her timidity at meeting gatherings of people, her greatest interest was *people*. This interest in others was wholehearted and absorbing, and she possessed the instinctive faculty of making whomever she met feel important to himself as well as to her.

Although only eighteen she had a strong sense of her own dignity as an actress and the dignity of her profession. She loathed scenes, arguments and ostentation. Though, like Booth, she dreaded meeting new people, to those with whom she felt at home she was a sensitive and responsive companion. Setbacks, which might have altered the career of one less determined, left Katharine Cornell undaunted.

She was strongly intuitive and moody. Cheerfulness was often followed by deep despondency which, however, was a secret thing. Too essentially kind to inflict it on others, she took her depression off to some place where she could be alone with it, and there, in solitude, she battled her way through.

She was and is devoid of professional jealousy. Tantrums were as foreign to her as wings. She was unfailingly generous. As for precedent, she ignored it. The fact that a certain thing was not customary, made no difference. She would go ahead and do it despite the cries of those about her that "it has just never been *done!*"

Procrastination was one of her faults. In small matters she was apt to be capricious and vacillating. Intense loyalty was as much a part of her as the hairs on her head. She made few intimate friends, but those that she had she kept and cherished. Punctuality has always been a law with her, for she was brought up on her father's maxim: "You may never make a success of anything, but at least you can be on time." She was scrupulously neat. Hard candy, walking, movies, detective stories, getting out into the country near the sea or the mountains—these simple things she enjoyed.

At eighteen she was approaching womanhood in a world torn by tremendous conflicting forces. It was 1916. Two years previously the long antagonism between Germany and Russia had terminated in a declaration of war. Resenting all things German since those fearful days of 1871, France had been quick to ally herself with Russia. In consequence of this alliance, Germany had a single dominant thought—to get France out of the way and then proceed to conquer Russia. The only way to get at France was through Belgium, and England, having pledged herself to protect Belgium, came valiantly to the side of France and

Russia. The war was spreading rapidly throughout Europe.

There was peace only in America. Despite her sympathy with the Allies, America insisted that it was not her fight and she would not become embroiled in it. A gigantic struggle was going on overseas. Americans read of it and thanked God they were safely aloof. They had no radios, but their newspapers told them of one German conquest after another, of German outrages and barbarism which struck terror and disgust into the minds of right-thinking people everywhere. Americans were talking war and dreading it, and shouting down those who proclaimed that America must prepare, while the President was asserting that America was "too proud to fight." Only the theaters offered release from all this. Theaters were doing a tremendous business. Mrs. Fiske was achieving new glories in "Erstwhile Susan" at the Gaiety. John Galsworthy's new play, "Justice," was thrilling its audiences at the Candler; even Shakespeare was drawing packed houses. Crowds were filling the Century to see "The Tempest," while the Lyric was doing excellent business with William Faversham in "Othello."

Though Kit was enjoying her work at the Comedy, she had one friend in New York who was convinced she was ready for bigger things. Mrs. Frances M. Wolcott, originally from Buffalo, had been one of Alice Cornell's friends. She was a cosmopolitan of wide interests, and in Buffalo each Sunday evening she had gathered interesting people together for mutual entertainment and stimulation. Even when Kit was younger, returning home for vacations, Mrs. Wolcott had considered her a promising personality, and invited her to these Sunday evenings. It was Alice who had persuaded her daughter to go, though Kit was years younger than any of the others, and was overwhelmed with shyness every time she went.

When Mrs. Wolcott came to New York, she looked Kit up at once. And since Winthrop Ames was one of Mrs. Wolcott's great friends, she gave Kit a letter to him. Though Ames had nothing for her, Mrs. Wolcott did not give up trying. She was a middle-aged, decisive, vigorous woman, the widow of Senator Ned Wolcott of Nevada, and in New York, as in Buffalo, she had a wide circle of acquaintances. She, too, loved everything theatrical, and was firmly convinced that Kit had real talent.

According to Mrs. Wolcott, the only trouble with Kit was that she did not know how to "push herself"; she lacked self-confidence, and what was more, she had not met the right people. All she needed to get ahead, Mrs. Wolcott maintained, was the right contacts. There were, for instance, those delightful people, the Favershams—Bill and Julie. She would give a dinner inviting those whom Kit ought to know—the Favershams; Cyril Harcourt, the actor; Robert Edmund Jones, famous designer of stage settings; John Corbin, then drama critic of the New York Times, and Mrs. Corbin.

Kit was not so enthusiastic about this as the older woman had expected. Though she politely assured Mrs. Wolcott that of course she would be happy to come, the prospect terrified her. To meet all these new people—all those important people! The idea made her miserable for days. She loathed parties and she still felt painfully ill-at-ease when meeting strangers. It did not help matters to realize that Mrs. Wolcott was arranging this dinner with the sole hope that Kit would impress these personages. To know that one is expected to impress others puts one at a disadvantage at the outset, and no lamb was ever led to the slaughter in greater torture than that experienced by Kit Cornell as she donned her dark green velvet dinner gown and set forth for Mrs. Wolcott's apartment.

Her hostess seated Mrs. Faversham on Kit's right. The talk was clever, swiftly paced, and gay. Outwardly, Miss Cornell was having a lovely time. Inwardly she was wondering how soon she could announce that she must leave for the theater. After the dinner had already seemed to have become part of eternity, she reminded herself that it could not possibly last more than an hour longer—and reached for a piece of bread.

Then it happened. She knocked a whole glass of burgundy into Mrs. Faversham's lap!

There was nothing to do except mumble an apology, sop up the wine, long desperately for extinction while Mrs. Faversham laughed and told her not to worry about it at all.

Later, in the taxi on the way to the Comedy, she closed her eyes and sighed. What an evening! What a nightmare! She had shamed Mrs. Wolcott, and the Favershams would never want to see her again. She sat, berating herself mercilessly for her clumsiness, exaggerating the episode in her own mind until it assumed the proportions of something catastrophic.

With the coming of summer the Comedy Theater closed, to reopen in early fall, and Kit was now so much a part of the organization that she was asked to return. She was grateful for this opportunity, grateful for the chance to play small parts, bad parts, any parts. She had no fatuous belief that stardom was just around the corner. Even at this early stage in her career, she had decided that the star system was wrong, anyhow. The play, she reasoned, was the paramount thing. No part in it was unimportant. The play must come first. A star, however brilliant, in a bad play with an inadequate cast could never sustain an audience. This idea, which she carried back home when she returned to Buffalo on vacation, was fixed and ineradicable.

Her father, a little stouter, a little balder, was only amused by his daughter's plunge into theatricals. "Wait," he said knowingly, "wait till you get a taste of real work. Wait till you find out what one-night stands are. Life has always been pretty easy for you, but wait till you have to go around to the agencies day after day. Then you'll change your tune. It's all new to you now, Kit, it's all strange and exciting—but wait!"

"That," she answered firmly, "is what I'm prepared to do—wait and work. It doesn't matter how long I wait and it doesn't matter how hard I work."

"You'll have to take a lot," he warned her.

She smiled. "I'm ready for what comes."

Despite the twenty-seven years difference in their ages, between these two now was growing a close companionship, a real understanding. During Kit's childhood, her father had been a strict disciplinarian, but now they could laugh and talk together like good friends.

She had been home only a few days when a telegram arrived. She read it—and read it again.

In spite of Kit's spilling burgundy down the front of his wife's dress, William Faversham was wiring Katharine

Cornell the offer to try out for the lead in his new play!
She, who had had less than a year of experience, was being
offered the opportunity to play the lead opposite one of the
foremost stars on Broadway. She could not understand it,
for as far she knew he had never been to see any of the performances at the Comedy.

She sat down quietly and thought the situation over.
She wanted to be very wise. Obviously, there were two
things she could do next season—she could go back to the
Washington Square Players, playing bits or anything she
was cast for, or she could try out for the lead with Faversham. Being Faversham's leading woman would mean
prestige and a salary of a couple of hundred dollars a week.
It was an alluring offer. Even well-known actresses were
eager for such a chance. But Katharine Cornell was concerned only with the question: Am I ready for this yet?
Am I prepared for such a big part? It took wisdom and
caution far beyond her years to wire Faversham a refusal.

Summer over, Aunt Lucy and Kit, with a friend from
Oaksmere, took an apartment on Forty-ninth Street. For
her second season Kit received forty dollars a year—twenty
dollars paid twice during the season.

It was 1917 and on April 6th, despite the supposed protective expanse of the Atlantic Ocean, an unprepared
America at last became part of the war. The country was
mobilizing rapidly. The young men of the Washington
Square Players were apt to be drafted any day. Changes
were inevitable. They held frequent meetings to discuss
what was to be done in the future. Undoubtedly some of
the men would be called into action with the United States'
forces, and undoubtedly some of them would not return.

Then what? They must all look ahead. They talked of forming a new organization after the war, an organization which would be called the Theater Guild. It was now May, 1917, and the Washington Square Players did not dissolve until the following year. But meanwhile meetings were being held and Kit was invited to attend them.

There was a particular Sunday night when a meeting had been called at the house of Lawrence Langner. One of the founders of the Washington Square Players, Langner was not only a member of an International Patent Law firm, but he was also a playwright. The room was crowded. Everyone was earnest, everyone was loquacious, everyone had ideas, and everyone's ideas were discussed lengthily. Money—how to raise it. Plays. Repertory.

The only member of the group who did not join in the arguments was a stranger, a pale young man, rather frail-looking, Kit thought. He sat across the room from her, smoking quietly, his eyes upon each speaker in turn, but his face expressionless.

Kit noticed him, although he seemed not to notice her at all. His silence made him outstanding in that volatile group, and she wondered who he was and why he had been included among them.

Finally someone turned to him, asking heatedly, "Don't you agree? Don't you think that's right?"

"No," he answered calmly, "I don't."

A sudden hush fell upon the gathering. Everyone stared at him. He met their eyes composedly.

A girl's voice broke the silence. "But why? Why don't you think so?"

Then he told them. He seemed to be speaking scarcely

more than a minute, but in that short time he covered every question which had been raised during the evening. And in a quiet, logical way he pointed out the flaws in their arguments and suggested in each case a wise solution.

"Who is that man?" asked Kit of someone near by.

"Don't you know who that is? He's the casting director for Winthrop Ames—Guthrie McClintic."

Rather a nice name, she thought. It sounded strong and important. But, after all, to a young girl seeking advancement on the stage, a casting director *was* important. Nine out of ten other young actresses would have made it their business to meet him and, if possible, impress him, but Kit Cornell walked back to the apartment on Forty-ninth Street only *thinking* about him. She had not seen him when she called at the Ames office with Mrs. Wolcott's letter. Quite apart from the fact that he was a casting director, Kit decided he would be an interesting person to know.

Romance had as yet no place in her life. She was not concerned with men. She was concerned with her career, and she was unbelievably happy. Each day she kept telling herself how wonderful it was to be an actress, to study new parts, to characterize them, to rehearse, to take curtain calls, to talk shop with her associates. Existence without acting in it was unthinkable.

She did not look like the accepted idea of an actress. There was nothing flashy about her. Seeing her on the street, one would not have noticed her particularly. She dressed simply, choosing costumes of dark colors and of crisp, straight lines. Her long hair, without even a wave in it, was drawn straight back from her face, and she used no make-up. Though jewelry was fashionable, she wore none of it, not even a ring, because she did not like jewelry.

One night toward the close of the season when she was playing in "Neighbors," a one-act play of Susan Glaspell's, a knock came on her dressing room door and she opened it to exclaim joyously, "Why, Miss Bonstelle!"

Miss Bonstelle, looking chic as always, grinned and said, "Hello."

"Come in. Oh, I'm so glad to see you. Were you out front?"

"Yes, I was. Well, Kit, you've grown up, haven't you? I made you a promise a long time ago, remember?"

"You mean—"

"I said that when you grew up you could work for me. How'd you like to go back to Buffalo and work this summer?"

"I'd love it!"

"Okay, then. Fifth business at fifty dollars a week."

"Oh!"

"Report for rehearsals June 20th at the Star Theater. I've already wired your father. I said, 'Thinking of engaging one Katharine Cornell for coming season.' Here's his answer."

Kit took the telegram and read:

"Are you crazy?
                    Peter Cornell."

They laughed, and then, quite serious, Kit said, "I need stock. There's no finer training in the world."

"Yes, that's true, up to a certain point. All young people breaking into the business need at least two or three seasons of stock. It means work, Kit, and when I say work, I mean work!"

CHAPTER SIX

KIT LEARNS A LESSON

*F*EMININE MEMBERS of the better stock companies included a leading woman, a "heavy" woman (sometimes termed "second business"), an ingénue, a character woman, and a woman who did "fifth business." The fifth woman belonged to none of the other four categories. She was expected to play anything—a French maid one week, an aged crone the next. The parts of the fifth woman were seldom long and seldom important. In the smaller, cheaper companies these parts were usually cut out entirely.

One of the biggest problems confronting the stock actress was that of clothes. Among the first questions asked by managers when engaging for stock was, "How's your wardrobe?" There were plays which required a complete change of costume in each of the three or four acts, and it was the unbreakable rule that so long as one played in the same town, one could never wear the same hat, coat or dress for more than a single week. Kit discovered that, financially, the engagement was a total loss, for not only was she spending every penny on wardrobe, but she was even going into debt for clothes. While some stock actresses could save money by making their own clothes, re-trimming hats, re-modeling dresses so that they could not be recognized, Kit had no knack for sewing. Too, if an actress could show off clothes to advantage, sometimes one of the local dress shops lent her gowns for a week in exchange for a couple of passes or a credit line on the program, but unfortunately for Kit the storekeepers of Buffalo did not regard her as the type they were seeking to model their fashions.

But as Miss Bonstelle had said, stock was splendid train· ing. It demanded versatility, adaptability and resourceful- ness. The world's greatest actors had served their appren- ticeship in stock—Ellen Terry, Henry Irving, Junius Brutus Booth, Edmund Kean, Samuel Phelps, Jo Jefferson, Mrs. Siddons, William Macready, Lawrence Barrett, Ada Rehan, Otis Skinner—the list is almost endless.

After playing fourteen weeks in Buffalo, the Bonstelle Company went to Detroit. Three times a week there was a matinee, every evening a performance. On matinee days rehearsal was called for ten in the morning and lasted often until twelve-thirty. When there was no matinee, it lasted all day. Between shows and rehearsals, parts must be studied and costumes planned. The leading woman was always given first choice of colors. It was considered a nice point of ethics for the other women to approach her during the earlier rehearsals asking what colors she was wearing in each act.

No one worked harder than did the indefatigable Jessie, who played leads. An excellent director, she permitted no slackening. She demanded discipline and got it. In the- atrical parlance the pages of a part are never called pages, but "sides." Most leading parts had from sixty to one hun- dred and twenty-five sides. There was only one week in which to memorize these. Night after night, the leading stock player sat up studying, a pot of black coffee at his hand, his head bound with a wet towel in order to keep awake. If he memorized readily, he was known as "a good study." If he found it difficult to memorize, he was a "bad study." Excessive study was termed "pounding," and at rehearsals one often heard the expression, "I've sure had to pound on that part"! There was a superstition, scoffed at by some stock actors, but religiously followed by others— if you slept with the part under your pillow, you would not have to "pound" it. Whether Miss Bonstelle adhered to this practice or not, she was "a good study."

She found "a good study" in Katharine Cornell. She found, too, someone pliable, ambitious, modest, eager for direction, ready for work. She found as well as remarkable talent, a strong and arresting individuality. From week to week she watched that talent unfold. This girl, she knew, had a future. She was not merely a young tyro enamored with something new.

While her initial reading of a part was always bad, Kit had a way of getting off by herself, thinking that part out, thinking it so intensely and so vividly that by the time the play went on she was able to submerge her own personality completely for that of the character which she was portraying. She had faults, but with conscientious work these could be remedied.

The summer season over, the company closed. The Washington Square Players were no more. Consequently when Kit returned to New York in that early fall of 1918, she began for the first time that wearisome business known professionally as "going the rounds."

Her fellow actors and her own burning interest and industry had told her where all the offices were. At first it was merely a question of going to the offices of managers and agents, and registering. These places, especially the agents' offices, were usually crowded. They might each have been stamped out of an identical mold. The walls were covered with autographed photographs. There were benches along three sides of the room, while one entire end was barricaded with a wooden fence, waist high, in the center of which was a small swinging gate. Unless they were being interviewed for an engagement, few actors ever entered through that gate. At a desk behind the fence, isolated regally from the crowd, sat a Personage—sometimes an office boy, sometimes the assistant of the man who ran the office.

A newcomer approached this august Being with respect, and with a smile as jaunty as one could muster for the occasion, saying, "I'd like to register, please."

The Personage, his face schooled to stoniness, never under any circumstances responded to the smile—these were superior and smileproof beings. The newcomer was handed a printed slip and briskly told to fill it out. The slip asked one's name, height, age, weight, color of hair, address, phone number and experience. Having filled out the questionnaire, the applicant returned it to the Personage who remarked negligently that he would "be kept in mind." This was registering.

The words of the Personage, "I'll keep you in mind," were never regarded as promises, but rather as a form of dismissal. The slip would be filed away, and having registered, the applicant had accomplished only a minor part of his quest. He must return to those offices day after day, mingling with the crowd, gradually edging up to the railing, seeking to catch the eye of the Personage.

"Anything doing today?"

The answer was invariably the same, "Nothing today . . . nothing doing today . . . come back in two weeks . . . sorry, nothing today . . ."

Fortunately these offices were clustered in a comparatively small area. At that time, the majority of them were from Fortieth Street to Forty-eighth Street, either on Broadway or a few steps to the east or west of it. Nevertheless, "going the rounds" required almost the entire day —from ten in the morning until about four-thirty in the afternoon.

Katharine Cornell was not spared this experience. She knew what it meant to come home at night footsore, weary even to the point of tearfulness, gallantly endeavoring, meanwhile, to reassure herself with the dogged insistence that it *must* come tomorrow. "It" meant a job.

It did not help to remind herself that hundreds of girls, prettier, with more experience than herself, were going through this identical ordeal. The offices were crowded with them, with girls of her own age—twenty. Some of them were shabby and making pathetic attempts to hide that shabbiness. Others were flashily dressed in satin with large picture hats and parasols. While others in suits, their trim skirts ankle length, their high-collared white shirtwaists spotless, looked like business girls.

Now and then on Broadway or in one of the offices, Kit would meet members of the Bonstelle Company or people who had been connected with the Washington Square

Players, and the glad news would be whispered: "They're casting up at Al Woods' office . . . or Chamberlain Brown's office . . . or at the Frohman office . . . or at the Packard Agency."

Let one office begin to cast, and the word flashed by unseen wires throughout all Broadway. The result was that within an hour the place would be so densely packed that actors would be compelled to congregate in the hallway.

To arrive while casting was in progress was a comparatively simple matter. It was now a question of waiting, sometimes for hours, and often with no place to sit. One leaned against the wall or shifted tiredly from one leg to another. Weariness was fought off desperately, for it would never do to *look* tired when one approached a manager.

Each office had its "pets." These privileged souls would elbow their way through the crowd, address the Personage by his first name, and be shown quickly into the sanctum sanctorum. But Katharine Cornell was not a "pet." To these offices she was as yet an unknown quantity. When at last she managed to reach the proximity of the railing she would be told, "No, you're not the type . . . you're too tall . . . you're too young . . . we're looking for a blonde . . ."

It was, she knew, all "in the game." She smiled very brightly, said "Thank you," and walked out into the street, her body aching and heavy with the weight of tears which she dare not shed. For it is the unwritten code on Broadway that one must keep smiling, one must never *appear* discouraged.

Seemingly all this had temporarily ended when Jessie Bonstelle phoned her one morning.

"How are you, Kit?"

"Oh—fine."

"Doing anything?"

"No."

"Well, I'm putting on a play for Grace George. There's a part in it I know you can do. Can you be at the Playhouse tomorrow at ten?"

"Yes, yes, I can, only—oh, Miss Bonstelle, you know I— I read so terribly!"

"Now, don't worry about that. I've seen you work. I know what you can do. You'll be all right. I'm directing. Don't worry. At ten then, the Playhouse."

Katharine Cornell hung up the receiver, her face burning, her hands icy. What a wonderful friend Miss Bonstelle was! While she blessed Jessie Bonstelle, she faced the prospect with dread. That awful first reading! And Grace George would be there, and perhaps Bill Brady, her husband, a brusque, short man with glasses who had been a prizefighter and was now one of Broadway's most successful managers. How could she go through with it? How? There were moments of sheer panic when she thought it would be easier to die.

There are actors who, given a part, are able to read it at once with smoothness and assurance, but Katharine Cornell was not one of these. Her first reading was always bad. No one was ever more conscious of his imperfections, and no one ever suffered more because of them than did Kit Cornell. Yet she was apparently calm as she approached the Playhouse on Forty-eighth Street next morning.

A group of actors had already assembled. Miss George was in the auditorium. Miss Bonstelle was near the footlights leaning over the wooden table on which were the manuscript and several blue-backed parts.

"Here you are, Kit," she said negligently, and handed Kit one of the small paper-covered books.

Inwardly trembling, Kit took it and walked off to one side. Her trepidation increased when she discovered that the play was a swiftly paced comedy. It was not her first attempt at such comedy, for she had played parts similar to this in stock. But this was not stock—this was Broadway production. If only she could have a little more time in which to familiarize herself with the lines! But she saw with dismay that she was on at the opening of the first act.

She listened to the stage manager as he explained the set, and then Miss Bonstelle said, "Okay, Kit, you're discovered at rise."

Kit read the part. It was almost as bad as that reading for the Washington Square Players two years before. Having finished her first scene, she made her exit, feeling suddenly limp. Miss George, dainty, blonde, an exquisitely feminine figure, was walking down the aisle. As she approached within the glow of the footlights, she beckoned to Kit. Keeping well to the side of the stage, out of the way of the rehearsing players, Kit approached the footlights and squatted above them.

Miss George spoke in a whisper, for the rehearsal was still going on. "You don't think you can play this part, do you, Miss Cornell?"

"I—"

"This sort of thing isn't your type. I can imagine you playing a more languorous part."

She walked back into the auditorium again, while Kit

moved wretchedly to the side of the stage. She *could* play that part! She knew it, but she interpreted Miss George's words as dismissal. Fight as she would against tears, they came, streaming down her face. There was only one thought now—to get away, to get out of the theater. Catching the eyes of the stage manager she beckoned to him. As he approached she reached the typewritten sheets toward him.

"What's the matter?" he asked concernedly.

"Miss George thinks I won't do."

She turned toward the stage entrance, stumbled down the long, paved alley at the side and, still crying, reached the street. Hopelessly, she wandered across Sixth Avenue, up to Fifth. The more she thought about the situation, the worse it became. And she told herself miserably that she must do something—anything—to get her mind off what had happened. In the midst of her despair, she remembered that a friend of hers had said she had a car in Washington and knew of no one who could drive it up to New York.

At times like this the nerves are so taut that physical action seems imperative, and the very thought of going all the way to Washington by train and driving her friend's car back to New York brought definite relief.

The trip required two days. By the time she returned to the city, she was calm and filled with fresh resolve. Dreadful as it had been, the episode at the Playhouse had already lost much of its sting.

It was well that she did not know what had taken place at the theater some few minutes after she had stumbled out of the stage door.

"We'll do that scene again," Miss George had said.

"But," answered the stage manager worriedly, "Miss Cornell isn't here. She's gone."

Jessie Bonstelle frowned. "Gone?" she gasped incredulously. "Gone?"

"Yes. She was crying, too. She said that Miss George thought she wouldn't do for the part."

"There!" Miss George turned to Miss Bonstelle. "There! You see? She hasn't the right stuff in her!"

Jessie Bonstelle was worried. The minute rehearsal ended, she hurried to a telephone. Kit was living in a small apartment on Fifty-seventh Street, and the boy at the switchboard told her that Miss Cornell had not yet come in.

"The minute she does, have her call Miss Bonstelle. It's important."

Three hours later she phoned again. "Did you give Miss Cornell my message?"

"Miss Cornell hasn't come in yet."

All next day Miss Bonstelle received the same answer. She remembered how the stage manager had said Kit was crying. Again and again, distractedly now, the older woman phoned.

"You haven't seen Miss Cornell? Hasn't *anybody* seen her?"

"No, madam. Miss Cornell has not been home."

"*Oh!*" gasped Jessie, and dire were the pictures that began haunting her.

Finally, before notifying the police, she made a last attempt.

"Hello," came a cheery voice.

"Kit! Where have you been for two days?"

"Oh, hello, Miss Bonstelle. I just got in. I found all your messages—"

"Where have you been?" thundered the older woman furiously.

"I drove a car up from Washington. Why?"

"Y-you—" Miss Bonstelle's voice sounded curiously weak, "you—drove—a car—up from—Washington?"

"Yes, I—"

"Well, of all the—you utter idiot! Why did you give up that part? How dare you leave rehearsal without being dismissed? Oh, if you knew what I've been through! I thought—I thought you'd done something dreadful! What else was I to think when I couldn't get you on the phone? Well, thank heaven you're safe. We've had to get another girl for the part, of course; but after you left . . ." she told Kit what had happened.

After replacing the receiver, Miss George's words rang like a challenge in Kit's ears. *"She hasn't the right stuff in her!"*

Katharine Cornell might have resented the assertion. She might have repudiated it with angry attempts at self-justification. But this is the weakling's way. Kit sat back quietly, realizing the justice of the accusation; realizing, too, that unpleasant though the experience had been, it had come to her because she needed this valuable lesson. Instead of resenting it, she was grateful for it and promised herself to remember it as long as she lived.

In order to emerge triumphantly out of the ranks of "just another actress," she must learn to stand fast, to take the bad with the good. She had known that she could play that part, yet she had been hurt, deeply hurt, at Miss George's words. She had foolishly resigned from the cast because she had leaped to the erroneous conclusion that she was not wanted. That was the straight of it. Could anyone, she asked herself, get ahead that way?

The thing to do was to keep trying and to keep hoping. Suppose she had stayed? Undoubtedly, her second reading would have been an improvement over the first—smoother, more fluent.

"Kit Cornell," she told herself firmly, "never again is a thing like that going to happen to you. It has been a lesson, but you won't need the same lesson twice. Never again will you run away—*from anything!*"

Once more the round of offices began, and once more this monotonous routine was interrupted by a telephone call from Jessie Bonstelle.

"Kit, Bill Brady's casting his third company for 'The Man Who Came Back.' The Mary Nash part—Marcelle—you've seen the show?"

"Yes."

"Would you like to try for it?"

"*Would* I!"

"All right. I've talked to the stage manager about you. You can rehearse with him privately for a while." She gave the address, and hung up with a cheery, "Good luck!"

"The Man Who Came Back" was under the management of William Brady and was one of the hit shows on Broadway that year. One company was still playing it in New York, while two other companies rehearsed for the road. A highly dramatic and doleful play, it depicted the story of a young man who degenerates through drink. The heroine, Marcelle, was a cabaret singer, desperately in love with the boy, and trying to save him from himself. Learning that he has been shanghaied, she goes to seek him in China where she, in turn, becomes a dope fiend. The big scene in the play is where the boy, crazed with drink, attempts to kill her.

Mary Nash, a dark, slim, intensely dramatic actress, had originated the part of Marcelle in the New York production. It was a part which, in common with every other young actress, Katharine Cornell was eager to play because, in theatrical vernacular, it was called "a swell *acting* part"— meaning that it ran the emotional gamut.

By the end of the week Kit knew the lines, and the stage manager was satisfied. Deciding that she was ready to rehearse with the company, he sent her to the theater Saturday morning.

The members of the company were unknown to her, as was the director, John Cromwell, a tall, thin, stern-looking young man with extraordinarily long legs.

Rehearsal went smoothly. Though a trifle self-conscious at first, Kit flung herself into the part. She loved it. Marcelle was as real to her as a living person. She had studied the lines diligently during the past week and was letter perfect in them. In time she would give a beautiful performance, but there was still much in the part that eluded her. It was characteristic of her that she should always reach out for nothing less than the highest in her performances. At twenty, she knew the meaning of Browning's thought in "Andrea del Sarto":

> "Ah, but man's reach should exceed his grasp,
>   Or what's a heaven for?"

Rehearsal over, she stood, waiting. There was a profound, and to her a seemingly eternal, silence. Cromwell stood, apparently meditating upon the fate of a universe. She began to feel uncomfortable. What was his verdict? Would she do? Had she been good? Would he fire her?

At length he raised his head and looked full at her. He had no need to call her to get her attention, Kit's luminous, heavily lidded eyes were fixed upon him eagerly.

"Could you play Marcelle at this afternoon's performance?" he asked unsmilingly.

She stared, her mind a strange medley of joy and uncertainty, of agitation, consternation and inspiration. Before she could answer, there was one phrase which kept churning in her head, "Opportunity knocks but once!" over and over again.

"Yes!" she said, and her voice had a ring of confidence.

As yet she had not known whether she was actually to play the part on the road or not. No contract had been signed, and this was her first company rehearsal. One way or another, this afternoon's performance would settle the matter. The manager and the director would be out front. The job hinged upon their decision.

Nothing unusual happened during the performance. The play ran smoothly, and when it was over the company congratulated her. Even better than this, however, was the notification from the management that the contract was waiting for her signature.

Five days later the tour began in Providence. This engagement was Katharine Cornell's first experience with "the road." The road meant sometimes catching trains at four o'clock in the morning in small towns where there

were no taxis at that hour. It meant battling her way with
a suitcase to the station through wind, rain, blizzards. It
meant one-night stands. It meant bad hotels, drafty dressing rooms, unappetizing food. It meant often sitting up
in day coaches all night. But she loved every minute of
it. Her salary was one hundred dollars a week, and though
expenses on the road were high, she managed to save a little
out of each week's salary.

The long tour left her unwearied, and no sooner was it
over than she reported for another season of summer stock
in Buffalo and Detroit with Jessie Bonstelle. Her salary now
was sixty dollars a week, for no longer was she doing fifth
business. Her parts now were second to those of Miss Bonstelle, herself—long parts which necessitated almost constant study.

She knew what tiredness meant when the season was
ended; her body was tired, her brain was tired. Her splendid
vitality had ebbed at last. All she wanted to do now was
rest. Rest seemed imperative. She thought longingly of the
tranquillity of Coburg, of stretching out upon the grass
under the trees, of stillness, of complete repose. No costumes to worry about for a while, no parts to study, no trains
to catch—just perfect, ineffable peace.

But the purposeful and energetic Miss Bonstelle had
other ideas.

CHAPTER SEVEN

KIT GOES TO LONDON

REST WAS a word which had no place in Jessie Bonstelle's vocabulary. Though she had just finished a strenuous summer season, she was already contemplating an ambitious fall production. It was now 1919. The war was over, and a blood-strewn, battered world was feverishly seeking to adjust itself to peace. Those who had fought for it proclaimed that it was a world which was safe—"safe for democracy."

As long as seven years ago, in 1912, Marian de Forest had dramatized Louisa M. Alcott's "Little Women." From office to office went the play on a seemingly unending pilgrimage. Fifteen managers read it, and fifteen managers, convinced that they knew what the public wanted, turned it down. Finally it reached the Brady office over the Playhouse Theater on Forty-eighth Street. There, at last, it found a receptive reader. Simple, plaintive, lovely, "Little Women" drew hordes of jaded, blasé New Yorkers into the Playhouse where they wept and laughed.

It was this highly successful play which Miss Bonstelle now decided to present in London with an all-English cast. The only American was to be Katharine Cornell who, she declared, was the ideal Jo. But Kit was frightened. Playing

Jo seemed a responsibility too great. She felt that she was not ready for anything so important as a London engagement, that she did not want to play Jo there, that she did not want to go there at all. Besides, she was tired.

"I need a rest. And anyhow, I may be right for Jo, but I'm not experienced enough for London."

Miss Bonstelle knew her fright, sensed her psychological withdrawing from too much responsibility, but she only smiled and said, "Nonsense. Pack your things right away. *We're going to London!*"

All weariness was forgotten the minute Kit read the part. She loved Jo. She loved the play. Jo was almost like another self—awkward, impulsive, tomboyish Jo.

She had thought she knew what rehearsing meant, but no rehearsals she had yet known were as difficult as these, for sometimes it seemed, not only to her but to the other members of the company, that Miss Bonstelle was unnecessarily severe. No one had ever worked harder than did Kit, but apparently it was impossible to please Miss Bonstelle. She would scold, ridicule, say harsh and caustic things in front of the others, make Kit go over scenes until she almost dropped. As far as Kit was concerned, she became a merciless tyrant. There were times when Kit sulked, times when she inwardly fumed, times when secretly she seethed with rebellion, times when she almost hated Miss Bonstelle, but she continued trying pathetically to please.

Even after the company opened in Manchester prior to its London showing, Miss Bonstelle did not relax in her efforts. Never did the final curtain fall but she would hurry around to Kit's dressing room, still hammering away at the girl.

"You must speak that line slower . . . In heaven's name, Kit, why do you hesitate before making the cross? . . . Play the scene further downstage . . . Why do you slouch like that? . . .

Finally even the members of the company began to resent it. One night in the hotel after the performance, when Miss Bonstelle had been unusually vituperative, the leading man, Leslie Faber, spoke his mind.

"Look here," he began, "it's none of my business, of course, but aren't you a bit harsh with Miss Cornell? You'll ruin the poor girl."

"I know what I'm doing."

"No, why don't you leave her alone? You'll only make her more self-conscious than she is. You'll destroy her individuality. Good Lord, how you rag her! I can't think how she stands it!"

Miss Bonstelle said nothing to justify her conduct, but Kit, who had chanced to overhear the conversation, began to wonder—had Faber hurt Miss Bonstelle? She could not bear the thought of her friend being hurt. She owed a great deal to Miss Bonstelle, and while she had chafed under the constant faultfinding, she realized that she had really benefited by it. Compassion, tenderness and gratitude filled her, and late as it was, she hurried down the hall and knocked at Miss Bonstelle's door.

"Please," she began, her voice so charged with feeling that it was not quite steady, "I—I just want you to know— I couldn't go to sleep without telling you—I don't mind, really. No, really, I don't. I know all you're trying to do and I'm grateful for what you *have* done. I—just wanted you to know that."

Miss Bonstelle looked at her a long time; then in a quiet, unhappy voice, she said, "Come in, Kit. Sit down."

Kit obeyed, and for a time there was only silence. She sat on the edge of the bed, the older woman took a chair facing her.

"Once," began Miss Bonstelle earnestly, "I was young like you. Once I, too, was just starting in this business; and once, like you, I wanted to be a really great actress—a Bernhardt, a Duse. Well, I'm no longer young. I've worked hard—and I've failed."

"You? Failed? Oh, no!"

"Yes. I'm a stock actress, that's all. Oh, it's true that now I'm directing Broadway productions and making good at it, but as an actress, Kit, I've failed. But you mustn't fail. I'm fond of you, very fond of you. I've known you ever since you were—that high. All that I've missed in the theater I want you to have. All that I've failed to do I want you to do. Do you understand?"

"Yes."

"I'm not young any more. I was never beautiful, and now I'm losing my figure. Oh, I'm not asking for sympathy, I just want you to know why I've kept at you and at you like I have. I'm not doing it for myself, but for you. I know what you need. I want you to be—not just another Broadway leading lady. I want you to be—no, even something more than a star. I want you to be—a truly great actress!"

"You think I can be—someday?"

"I believe in you implicitly. I know actors, my dear. I know acting. I know what I'm talking about. I'm ambitious, not for myself any more, but for you. So, if I pick on you—"

"I'll thank you for it!"

Kit's eyes filled with tears. Never before had she fully realized how truly wonderful, how valiant Jessie Bonstelle was. She felt humble, and words with which to express her gratitude seemed suddenly bunglesome and inadequate.

With the London opening in November, it was evident that Jessie Bonstelle's hopes for "Little Women" had not been in vain. Londoners poured their money into the box office. London critics were kind, especially to the American girl who was giving such an inspired performance of the ever-lovable Jo.

The play an established success, Miss Bonstelle returned to New York. Appearing in London nowadays does not necessarily further the career of American actors. A hundred years ago the best actors on the American stage were—at least in the opinion of the American audiences—those who came from England. Rightly or wrongly, American actors were prone to resent this attitude, and to increase their prestige in their own country, American stars journeyed to London seeking recognition there. Edwin Forrest, Charlotte Cushman, Edwin Booth, Joseph Jefferson and many others considered a London success necessary in order to strengthen their positions at home. This condition no longer prevails. Today, American stars are content with the laurels earned in their own country. Consequently, Katharine Cornell was not laboring under the opinion that this London success would prove an open sesame upon her return to New York.

She was, however, playing a leading part in a successful play. One expects an actress in such a position to be feted, courted. Such was not the case with Kit. She was very lonely, knew scarcely anyone, had no social life. Among the few friends that she made at this time was one friendship which was to prove long and enduring. Joyce Carey, who played Kit's sister, Meg, was ten years later to play Kit's sister again in "The Barretts of Wimpole Street."

Meanwhile Kit, loving golf, played it as often as possible. Her room was small and it was never warm enough.

Loneliness and homesickness were intensified when Christmas came. She spent the entire day alone in her chilly room and was glad when it ended.

A member of the company, realizing how desperately homesick she was, invited her to dinner one evening in January. "I know how much you Americans like corn," she said. "We never have it over here, at least not on the cob as you Americans eat it, but I've managed to get some ears of corn just for you!"

All next day Kit thought longingly of corn on the cob. It *would* seem like home!

"Corn?" she asked delightedly that night when a large dish was given the place of honor on the table.

"And exactly as you have it in America!" With an air of triumph, the proud hostess lifted the lid.

The corn had been sliced down the middle of the cob just as if it were cucumbers!

One day her telephone rang and a very feminine English voice asked if this were Miss Cornell.

"Yes."

"You don't know me, but an American chap who was here just before you came, asked me to call you and do what I could to make things pleasant for you."

"Oh? How nice. Who is he?"

"Guthrie McClintic."

For a moment Kit's brow knit in a puzzled frown. Mc-Clintic. McClintic. The name was familiar. McClintic. Then she remembered. Guthrie McClintic—of *course!* Lawrence Langner's house—the meeting of the Washington Square Players—that frail-looking, interesting young man who had set everyone on the right track so easily. Odd that he should have remembered her—very, very odd.

In February "Little Women" closed and Kit sailed for home. There would be a few months' rest and then playing stock leads in Detroit the coming summer. Beyond that, who knew?

Jessie Bonstelle was waiting on the dock. They waved gaily to each other, and when at length the interval with the customs was over and they were walking to the elevator, Jessie announced that they were going to have a new director for Detroit this season because she intended to have two companies and herself to remain almost entirely with the company in Buffalo.

"He's a young fellow named McClintic. Enormously clever. Ever hear of him?"

"Oh, yes," admitted Kit.

"Such a fine person. You'll like him."

Kit was quite sure of that.

CHAPTER EIGHT

LOVE

*L*ET OTHER boys talk about baseball, Guthrie Mc-
Clintic was interested only in the theater. His father, Edgar
D. McClintic of Virginia, could not understand this. Why
should his son be different from other boys? Why must he
be thinking theater, talking theater, wanting to go to the
theater all the time? According to the elder McClintic, this
sort of thing would not get the boy anywhere. But no
parental lectures had the slightest effect upon young Mc-
Clintic's love for the stage.

Born in Seattle, Washington, on August 6, 1893, he was
five years older than Kit. Even in his early teens, he was an
enthusiastic patron of the old Grand Theater on Cherry
Street between Second and Third, and the Moore Theater
on Second and Stewart Streets where he saw every play that
came to Seattle. To do this out of his pocket money meant
denying himself things which to other boys were important.
Though he could never afford seats anywhere but in the
top gallery, he saw the best actors and actresses of the day,
including Bernhardt, Modjeska, Mrs. Fiske.

By the time he had entered Lincoln High School at fifteen, he had made up his mind to be an actor. While his

fellow-pupils were discussing their splendid football team, the "Lynx," young McClintic was thinking about the last play he had seen. A small, lonely figure, he would walk for hours along the broad, clean streets lined with maples, past tidy frame colonial houses set back in neat yards, dreaming of the day when he would be speaking lines on a real stage. His father hoped that this was merely something which he would outgrow, but it lingered with him tenaciously all through high school. After six months at the University of Washington, Guthrie McClintic packed his bag for New York and the American Academy of Dramatic Art.

His career actually began at the age of twenty when in August of 1913 he became assistant stage manager for a play produced by Winthrop Ames called "Her Own Money," a job which materialized through the simple procedure of writing Ames a letter requesting an interview.

Ames was quick to recognize ability and quick to appreciate ambition. Producing "The Great Adventure" later that year, he entrusted the stage management to McClintic, thus it was McClintic who rang up the first curtain of the Booth Theater, for the theater had just been built.

Even at this early stage of his career, McClintic had realized that it was directing he loved, rather than acting, and it was toward this goal that his attention was now focused. The following year, though he was but twenty-one, he was not only stage manager, not only playing a small part, but casting director for Ames' new production, "The Truth." It was a genuine responsibility to be given to one so young and one so new in the business, but there was something about this boy, even then, which inspired confidence. His salary, however, was only thirty dollars a week. By 1916 he

was Ames' production assistant, which brought him a step
nearer his dreamed-of goal.

Now, in 1920, at twenty-seven, he had behind him seven
years of uninterrupted service in the theater. He had taken
this stock engagement with Jessie Bonstelle because, though
his place was already achieved in theatricals, he realized
that stock experience would give him a more complete
equipment. The season was to last for seventeen weeks,
which meant that in that time he would be called upon not
only to act in, but to produce, seventeen plays, since Miss
Bonstelle planned to spend most of her time that year in
Buffalo.

The company for Detroit that season included Gilda
Varesi and Frank Morgan, a talented young actor, now
elevated to his first stock leads.

Guthrie McClintic had already fallen in love with Katharine Cornell, and it did not take Katharine Cornell longer
than a single week to fall head over heels in love with
Guthrie McClintic.

Before that first week had ended, every member of the
company was of the opinion that this hardworking young
director was a lovable personality. He was unfailingly frank,
yet his frankness never took the form of brutality since, even
then, he had founded his direction upon that which was
constructive rather than destructive. He was the sort who
never forgot a friend and never forgot the kindnesses shown
him. Everybody liked him. He had many splendid gifts—
the gift for making friends readily, the gift of being an interesting conversationalist, the gift for repartee, the gift for
story-telling, the gift for expressing himself freely, and

although he would never admit it, he had written poetry as a boy. His love for poetry was surpassed only by his love for all that was high and beautiful in the theater.

Though only twenty-seven, he appeared even younger. This quality of seemingly perpetual youth would remain with him, an attribute inextinguishable, for Guthrie McClintic was possessed of that rare characteristic—a youthful spirit. He had a naturally happy disposition. He believed in everybody, and everybody, somehow, believed in him. He was an idealist; his ideals animated him, spurred him, sustained him. Cheapness disgusted him. He loved luxurious surroundings, rich colors, fine silver. Even then he had a clearly defined ideal of the theater and his part in it, and steadfastly he refused to lower his ideals. The theater was at once his love, his joy, and his despot.

Of medium height, with a light complexion, a well-shaped head and a fine brow, he had the friendliest eyes in the world. He walked quickly, and there was a bouyancy about his step. He was not, however, an athlete. Though active, energetic, capable of sustained effort and great endurance, physical exertion had no appeal for him.

Unlike other girls of twenty-two, Kit had never been in love before. She had had no time for it. Her work had absorbed and satisfied her. Marriage was something about which she had thought little. Long ago she had determined that nothing should interfere with her career. But loving Guthrie was as inevitable as sunlight; besides, it was different from falling in love with someone whose interests lay outside her own sphere of activity. For him as well as for her this stock engagement was only the beginning. They understood each other, each respecting, each treasuring, the aims of the other. They knew they could work together without conflict, helping each other, both striving for perfection in the art of the theater. Neither knew what the future might hold, but they knew they could face it the more gallantly, facing it together.

McClintic told her one day that he had been in love with her for exactly four years. She laughed at this, it was just another of his delightful whimsicalities.

"No," he insisted, "it's true. It was while you were playing in 'Plots and Playwrights.' That was when I first saw you!"

"But you didn't know me then!"

"That didn't matter. I was scouting for talent for Ames, and I dropped in at the Comedy one night. And there you were."

"Heavens, what a rank amateur I was then!"

"Yes, but sitting in the darkened theater, I scribbled a note to myself. Would you like to know what it said?"

"I dare you to tell me!"

"I wrote three words: 'Interesting; monotonous; watch.' And then I saw you at Langner's, of course; and then I saw you standing in the Brady office one day just recently. The place was crowded and I don't suppose you noticed me at all. At least, you didn't seem to see me."

"I didn't."

"Well, I saw you, all right, and when I met Olive Wyndham later, she asked me why I was so thoughtful. I said: 'You know, Olive, it's a strange thing to say, but today I saw the girl I'm going to marry. I don't know her yet, but I know that someday we'll be married!'"

Someday we'll be married. Lovers have said it since time

began. Someday we'll be married; but for Guthrie and Kit, wonderful and beautiful as love was, it was a love which had to be shared with that which was the first love for both of them—the theater. And the demands of the theater were insistent, remorseless, unending. Script followed script. Part followed part; longer parts than ever now for Kit, who was playing leads; new, untried scripts for Guthrie. It was hot in Detroit that summer, yet one must disregard the heat. One must study all the time, everywhere.

"I love you, Kit."

"I love you, too, darling. Look, would you mind cueing me in that last scene? It's so terribly tricky. Do you think I could wear a cape in the first act? Capes are so smart this year. Or do you think a suit would be more in character?"

For McClintic the work was even more difficult than for Kit, for he must not only familiarize himself with the scripts beforehand in order to direct them, but he was playing parts as well.

Miss Bonstelle, who alternated between Buffalo and Detroit, was worried. "Don't tell me you and Guthrie are falling in love?" she asked one day.

Kit laughed. "Falling in love? We are in love!"

Jessie tucked in a wisp of her red hair nervously. "Don't be a fool," she begged. "You've your career to think about. It's utterly ridiculous for you to be thinking about marriage just now. I've known girls who have worked quite as hard as you have worked, girls who have shown the same bright promise—and then they fell in love. What happened? They married—and nobody ever heard of them afterward. If you want to get ahead, my dear, the theater's got to come first."

"It does. It always will—with both of us."

"That's what you think *now*."

But it was evident, even to Miss Bonstelle, that though McClintic was in love with Kit, this fact did not cause him to spare her at rehearsals. His well-modulated voice interrupted her scenes as often as it did those of Gilda Varesi or Frank Morgan or any of the others.

There was a time when in a particularly dramatic scene, Kit was supposed to scream.

"It's wooden, Kit," he called out. "Try it again."

Again she screamed.

"No, no, that won't do. Try once more. Take the scene from the beginning."

Wearied to the point of exhaustion, she kept on screaming, and he kept insisting that it was not the *right* scream. She was as determined as he that that scream should be right, but by now she was convinced that she could not please him.

"Yes," he maintained, "you *can*. Try it once more."

She screamed again, and he only shook his head. Finally he rushed toward her and purposely upset a heavy table. It hit her on the shin and she screamed with pain.

"There!" smiled McClintic, "now you've got it. That's exactly the way I want it to sound. Splendid, Kit! Do it just like that at the performance."

Many people—managers, critics, actors—were predicting a glorious future for this young man, and it did not take Katharine Cornell long to realize that he was a truly great director. She was as ambitious for his success now as she was for her own, and she took his direction eagerly, without questioning or argument.

All the elements necessary for an artistic director were

inherent in Guthrie McClintic. First, he was equipped with
splendid health, sound nerves and abounding energy. Naturally fearless, he dared to do in direction what other directors might fear to do. Away from the theater, he was impulsive. In the theater, this impulsiveness took the form of
sudden inspiration. Ideas poured through his mind at rehearsal, seemingly without any previous seeking for them
on his part. They were suddenly there and he trusted them.
He knew things without knowing how he knew them. Another quality necessary to successful direction is taste.
Where stage productions were concerned, McClintic's taste
was excellent. Too, he was ambitious and enthusiastic.
Though he was fond of luxury and loved ease, he considered
no amount of work too great to achieve the effect he
wanted. He permitted no one to dictate to him. He had to
carry out his ideas in his own way. Insight, another vital
requisite for a director, was pronounced in him. He had
insight, not only in regard to the actor whom he was directing, but also in regard to the character which the actor
portrayed. His judgment in everything theatrical was sound,
and already his associates had learned to have implicit faith
in it.

It did not take Kit long to understand him. Unlike herself, in whom there was a strong trait of caution, McClintic
did things on the spur of the moment. Though he was
quick to anger, his anger evaporated even more readily than
it was aroused, and there were no sulks afterward. It was
impossible for him to hold a grudge.

Had anyone asked Kit what it was she most admired in
this man, it would have been difficult for her to answer. One
day she would have said it was his warmheartedness; an-

other time she would have said it was his stanchness to
his friends, or his abiding faith in her; another day she
would have said that what she most admired in him was
his natural love, talent and enthusiasm for the theater.

They had little time to talk of themselves, little time for
lovemaking. Occasionally, when the weather permitted and
the parts were lighter than usual, they strolled in Grand
Circus Park after the performance. There was a certain
bench which they called "our" bench, and they would walk
toward it hurriedly, hoping that it would be empty. It
invariably was. There they would sit for hours talking of
what they meant to do in the theater. The end of the
Detroit season would mean "going the rounds" for Kit, but
McClintic would return to the Ames office, no longer as
casting director, but to assist in the stage direction of the
contemplated production of "The Green Goddess" which
was to star an English actor named George Arliss. Too, he
had the prospect of having an entire production entrusted
to him, for so great was Ames' faith in him that Ames had
offered to supply the capital to back any play which Mc-
Clintic might consider worth while. Together, on "their"
bench, they dreamed lofty dreams of how, one day, Guthrie
would produce plays of their own choosing, and she would
act in them.

But the intervals on the bench were rare. Work was so
hard that toward the end of the seventeen weeks, Kit
wondered whether she would be able to finish the season.
At length the end was in sight—only two more weeks, only
two more plays—"Lombardi, Ltd." and "Civilian Clothes."

It was Monday night. The script for "Civilian Clothes"
had come, and "Lombardi, Ltd." had opened. As they left

the theater, McClintic suggested hiring a car and riding around Belle Isle. The hours' ride would be restful for both of them.

In the car they discussed marriage, two very rational young people determined that for them marriage would *last*. Kit argued that they must be very, very sure. To her, marriage was a serious and sacred thing. Here in Detroit, she reasoned, they had been thrown almost constantly together for seventeen weeks, but New York might make a difference. Suppose one day after they returned to the metropolis, Guthrie should look at her with that "what-did-I-ever-see-in-you" expression. No, she argued, they must wait. A year at least. Meanwhile, they would both be perfectly free.

McClintic left it at that. He was sure of himself, but he knew that Kit must be sure, too.

The ride over, he suggested scrambled eggs and coffee at Thompson's. They left the car at the Boulevard, walked a block and a half through the now silent streets, entered the restaurant and gave their orders. Just as the waiter was placing the dishes, McClintic's face took on an expression of horror.

"*Good heavens!*" he cried.

Alarmed, Kit gazed up at him.

"The script!" he explained. "I've left the script in the car!"

This was catastrophe. The car was not even a taxi. It was just a dark, ordinary cruising car, and they had not noticed it particularly nor had they paid any attention to the driver. A lost script! And rehearsal called for ten o'clock in the morning!

"Could you put in a long distance call to the New York office for another script?" she asked.

"No, that's impossible. The office wouldn't be opened at this time of night, and to wait until morning means that it would be at least two days before a new script could get here."

And the play opened next Monday! She moaned. What would Miss Bonstelle say? She would be furious. She would say, of course, they had lost the script through carelessness, because they were in love. Wretchedly, hopelessly, they gazed at each other.

Because there seemed nothing else to do, Kit reached for her coffee, sipped it. McClintic sat there staring down bleakly at his eggs.

All of a sudden Kit had the curious feeling that something was tugging at her, some power within herself, insistent and irresistible, was urging her to rise. Before she realized what she was doing, she had put down her coffee cup and started for the door.

"Let's go," she cried, "—now!"

Wonderingly, McClintic threw some change on the table and followed. They almost ran the block and a half back to the Boulevard. The street was empty, silent. A lone policeman saw two well-dressed, wild-eyed young people racing along, not speaking to each other. A solitary car passed them, but they paid no attention to it. Then they heard the honk of a horn, and a voice called out: "Hey! Want 'nother ride?"

McClintic muttered something unintelligible, yanked open the door, pulled out the manuscript. Had they left Thompson's a few seconds later the car would have been gone! Rehearsal for "Civilian Clothes," the last play of the season, began promptly next morning.

There was nothing to worry about now but New York. McClintic would help produce "The Green Goddess" and hunt for a play of his own. Kit would look for a job.

Instead of acting as a wedge between them, New York drew them even closer together. On the 8th of September—Katharine Cornell never forgot the date—McClintic took her dancing on the Pennsylvania Hotel Roof. Just before leaving they wandered out upon the balcony. Below them the fabulous, teeming city that was New York glittered like a million topazes; behind them they could hear the orchestra playing "Whispering," the hit tune of the year.

"Whispering that I—love—you—" ran the chorus.

Guthrie McClintic was whispering the same thing. He had directed dozens of love scenes, she had acted in dozens of them, but never had they imagined anything quite so solemn and so exquisite as this moment.

When they left the Pennsylvania Roof that night they were definitely engaged. McClintic's salary had just been raised to one hundred and twenty-five dollars a week. To friends and family they gaily announced their engagement.

None of Kit's family approved. Her father was frankly against it. Mrs. Wolcott exclaimed, "But, my dear child—marriage! It's absurd. It will ruin your career."

Jessie Bonstelle argued lengthily and vehemently. "It's not that I haven't confidence in Guthrie," she insisted. "I have. There's something about him that inspires confidence. It isn't that. I like Guthrie personally, but I just don't think he's the right man for you, and I believe that marriage will jeopardize your career."

None of this made the slightest impression upon Kit.

They did not know when they would be married. There were things they each wanted to do, first. McClintic still had to find his play and produce it. Kit still had to find a job—that ever-elusive job.

And it was a long, long hunt. September. October. November. December. January. February. March. Always meeting the same tedious responses: "Mr. Woods isn't casting . . . Mr. Selwyn's out of town . . . Mr. Harris isn't seeing anybody . . . Nothing today . . . Come back in two weeks . . . Nothing doing today . . ." Seven months of it.

She had been five years on the stage, and seemingly she was as far as ever from a Broadway production. Knowing what she was going through, McClintic was suffering with her, but he was helpless to remedy the situation. Hopefully, he introduced her to Winthrop Ames when Ames began casting for "The Green Goddess."

Ames, a tall, slender, sharp-featured man, immaculately groomed, looked her over with a cold and speculative glance. "If you could have your choice of every part ever written, Miss Cornell, which would you choose?" he asked.

Fired at her with such abruptness, the question found Kit at a loss. She knew that he expected her to name something like Juliet, but she could not bring herself to say that because it would not have been honest; she did not want to play Juliet. Besides, after hunting for work so long, any part would have been desirable.

"All I want is a job," she told him feelingly.

"I see," he answered frigidly, and began fingering some papers on his desk.

When she had left he turned to McClintic. "That girl has no ambition," he declared.

Knowing Kit, McClintic's face flushed with anger. It was characteristic of him that he would take any slight to himself with commendable equanimity, but he would fiercely resent it for her.

One day in late March, Kit's telephone rang.

"Miss Katharine Cornell?" asked a businesslike, feminine voice.

"Yes, this is she."

"Well, this is Miss Humbolt of the Packard Agency. Could you get down here right away?"

Miss Humbolt was a tall, thin, severely gowned, severely browed, middle-aged woman who wore glasses, used no make-up, and looked more like a strait-laced, old-fashioned, small-town school marm than a theatrical agent. To Kit, knowing that this was a call for work, that cold, metallic voice had the dulcet tones of an angel.

Katharine Cornell did not know it then, but at last her days of tramping from office to office were ended.

CHAPTER NINE

MARRIAGE—AND "A BILL OF DIVORCEMENT"

*R*ACHEL CROTHERS, a clever playwright whose plays almost without exception were successful, was casting for a new play called "Nice People." Miss Humbolt sent Kit to see Miss Crothers for the part of Eileen Baxter-Jones, a wisecracking, sophisticated society girl. Having interviewed Kit, the author decided that though she was not the type, still she had "a kind of distinction," and she would let her try it.

Kit was happy. It did not matter that the part was small. It was a job. And next to Guthrie, a job was the most important thing in the world.

But on the morning for which the first rehearsal had been called, Kit awoke feverish, dizzy, her throat aching, and scarcely able to talk.

"Well, young lady," announced the doctor, "looks like you're coming down with diphtheria."

Diphtheria! Kit groaned. If she *had* to have diphtheria, why—oh, why did she have to have it just *now*? There had been seven months of idleness in which she could have had diphtheria, and now, just when at last she had a part—

"Of all the rotten luck!" she fumed.

It did not matter particularly that the next day the doctor changed his mind and called it quinsy, and told her that she would have to have her tonsils out.

She sighed dismally. "Well, all right. I've lost the job, anyhow, so I might as well have my tonsils out as soon as possible."

For weeks Kit was unable to leave the apartment, but once on the way to recovery, she gained strength rapidly. She knew that she was going to need plenty of strength, for now there seemed nothing ahead but the dreary prospect of tramping from office to office again.

She was sitting by the window one day when Guthrie came. "The Green Goddess" had been produced and was a hit, and now he was reading script after script searching hopefully for that one which would merit his launching out as a producing manager on his own account.

"You know," he said, "I don't believe the Crothers play has gone into rehearsal, after all. I haven't heard a thing about it. It looks as if it might have been postponed for some reason."

Kit leaned forward, suddenly well. "You mean there might still be a chance? Oh, Guthrie, that's marvelous! What shall I do? Shall I write to her?" and then without waiting for his reply, "Yes, I'll write right away and you can mail it as you go out!"

It seemed too good to be true that something could have held up the production of "Nice People" until she was well again, but this was confirmed when Miss Crothers' reply brought the request that Miss Cornell should report for rehearsal on Wednesday.

"Nice People" was a sophisticated play of bright, clever

dialogue. The lead was played by an attractive little red-headed actress, Francine Larrimore, and Tallulah Bankhead, as yet unknown, played a small part. The play made one of the hits of the 1921 season. Kit's part, being small, created no particular attention. No one on Broadway had ever heard of her. But this could not dampen her happiness. She was on Broadway at last, and in a hit show. Who knew what might turn up for next season?

Guthrie, too, was happy. He had found the play he wanted, a play called "The Dover Road," and was planning to open it in December.

With the coming of the first warm days of spring, he and Kit would go out of town each Sunday to a quiet place she knew of in Mamaroneck. With them would be a basket containing lunch, and under Guthrie's arm the inevitable script, for he was still associated with the Ames office and although he had decided on his own play, it was part of his job to read other plays, even those which were to be produced during the coming season by managers other than Ames. So Sundays these two would go swimming, cook their lunch over an open fire, and when it was finished, Kit would stretch out in the sun, and Guthrie would read aloud the script he had brought, continuing to read as long as the light held.

On a particular Sunday in early June, he lit a cigarette and opened his manuscript. "This one's called 'A Bill of Divorcement,'" he announced. "I understand it has already made a big hit in London, and an English actor, Allan Pollock, has bought the American rights and intends to present it this fall under Dillingham's management. Well, ready, Kit? All set?"

She nodded, and he began reading. He had not read far before she sat bolt upright, tense with interest.

"This," she murmured, "is a play!"

"A Bill of Divorcement" required two leading women; the character lead, the mother, and the ingénue lead, the daughter, Sydney, which was far the better part.

"How I'd love to do Sydney!" she exclaimed.

But that was impossible and they both knew it. That she, unknown, now playing her first small part on Broadway, should have even a chance at such a role, was something for which one did not even dare hope. Nevertheless, listening to McClintic read, Kit could visualize herself playing that part.

"Who'll play it, I wonder?" she asked wistfully, when he had finished.

"I don't know. Ames told me Pollock has two plays, and he's planning to bring both of them to New York this fall. If the second one's as good as this—"

They could not stop talking about "A Bill of Divorcement." They talked about it long after the sun went down, talked about it all the way to New York and, unable to sleep, Kit thought about it long after she got into bed that night. Even next morning her first thought upon awakening was of Sydney. A few days later her mail brought a typewritten postcard from the Packard Agency which read: "We have had a cable from Allan Pollock in London. He asks will you be free in September. Please get in touch with this office at once."

She dashed to the phone and called McClintic, excitedly reading him the message. "What do you think it means, Guthrie? What can it be? It can't be—Sydney?"

How had Pollock heard of her? She had not met him during her stay in London. No, it couldn't be Sydney, of course. That would be too much of a miracle. Things like that just did not happen. She told herself that she must be calm about this, that it was some mistake.

"Well, you remember I told you that Pollock had two plays?"

"You think then—" her voice sank with disappointment, "it isn't 'A Bill of Divorcement' at all? You think it's the other play?"

"Well, there are only four feminine parts in 'A Bill of Divorcement'—the mother, a maiden aunt, Sydney, and a maid, which is only a bit. You couldn't play the mother. You certainly couldn't play the maiden aunt, and he wouldn't be cabling about the maid. So, obviously, it's either the other play or it's Sydney."

"It can't be. Not Sydney!"

"But why should Pollock cable about you, anyhow?"

"I don't know. And why should he cable at all unless it were some *important* part? I'll phone the Packard office right away and call you back!"

But the Packard office had no information at all. The only thing they had was Pollock's cable asking: "Is Katharine Cornell free September?"

The answer sped back: "Cornell free September what for?"

Kit was on tenterhooks, afraid to hope, trying to prepare herself for a disappointment, telling herself that Pollock must be thinking of some other Katharine Cornell. Waiting was agony. Next morning she called the Packard office, trying in vain to mask the agitation in her voice.

"Miss Humbolt, have you heard anything from Pollock?"

"No, we've had no answer yet. I'll call you the minute we know."

Mid-afternoon the reply came. Pollock's cable contained one word: "*Sydney.*"

The miracle had happened. To Kit, the whole thing seemed like some utterly fantastic dream. She was almost afraid to think too much about it, afraid to talk about it. The situation began to take on some semblance of reality, however, when a call came to report to the Dillingham office and see Fred Latham, the casting director.

Kit had not been in the office five minutes before she realized with dismay that neither Dillingham nor Latham thought her suitable for Sydney. And if they did not want her to play it, would Pollock be able to hold out against them? Might they not convince him that he had made a wrong choice? Oh, she mustn't lose Sydney, she mustn't! It was evident that Pollock had cabled Dillingham that he wanted her for the part and that Latham was interviewing her merely as the result of that cable.

"You've seen 'Nice People'?" she asked.

"Yes. Both Mr. Dillingham and myself caught the show."

That was it, then. That was the reason they did not want her for Sydney. It was because the hard-boiled Eileen Baxter-Jones was the direct opposite of the splendid, sympathetic part under discussion. They had arrived at the conviction that Eileen was her type of part and that she could not play any other kind. Well, she'd show them that she could—that is, if they would only give her the *chance* to show them! The manager and casting director combined to make a powerful force leagued against her. She knew that. Seeking to be just to them, she could even view the situation from the managerial standpoint. Sydney was really a star part. Undoubtedly, they wanted some "big name" to play it. As yet Kit did not comprehend why she was even being considered for the part, but the fear of losing it brought sharp despair. "Oh, God," she prayed wildly, "don't let them take it away from me!"

"What salary would you want to play Sydney?" asked Latham.

She hesitated. Only the day before she had talked this over with Guthrie. They both knew that if a "name" were playing it, a strong part like Sydney would pay at least four hundred dollars a week, and even as much as seven hundred. But Katharine Cornell was not yet a "name." They knew all about her in Buffalo and she was a favorite in Detroit, but this meant nothing to Broadway. With "Nice People" she was getting a hundred dollars a week, and actually, as Guthrie had said, she wanted to play Sydney so badly that she would have played it for nothing.

"Two hundred and fifty," she answered.

"Okay," answered Latham, and began toying with some papers on his desk.

A trifle dazed, Kit Cornell walked out of the office, knowing that her chances of playing Sydney were only about one to nine.

When Pollock arrived in America, it was almost a foregone conclusion that Latham and Dillingham would convince him that she was not suitable for the part. Well, she told herself grimly, she must school herself to face that.

Although she did not know it, cables were already flashing back and forth over the Atlantic from the Dillingham office to Pollock, but so far Pollock had stood firm. Meanwhile, there were two things Kit had to do. One was to resign from "Nice People." The other was to marry Guthrie.

The 8th of September, 1921, exactly one year after that evening on the Pennsylvania Roof, was the date set for the wedding. On the 3rd Kit left the cast of "Nice People" and took the train for Coburg, Ontario. At first she had decided that she and Guthrie would go quietly down to the New York City Hall and be married, but Aunt Lydia had other ideas.

"You must have your wedding in your own home!" she insisted. "It's probably the only wedding you'll ever have. Oh, dear, you still seem like a little girl to me. Why, it seems only yesterday that your father was taking away your roller skates for a week to punish you for having poured ink on that old brown leather chair in his office. And now—" her eyes were bright and beseeching, "you're very sure, Kit?"

"I was never more sure of anything in my life," Kit answered quietly. "Guthrie and I are getting married—for keeps."

When McClintic arrived for the wedding almost the first thing he told her was that rehearsals for "A Bill of Divorcement" would begin on the 9th! They had planned a short honeymoon, but this meant that they would have to rush back to New York immediately the wedding was over.

McClintic, who could assume command of vast productions, who could govern excitable actors with poise, wisdom and assurance, who could face the turmoil of dress rehearsals with an equanimity which seemed sometimes almost superhuman, was frankly nervous at the prospect of his own wedding.

On the day preceding the ceremony, in the lovely front room of the old Cornell house, he took part in a rehearsal at which he was not the director. He only owned two suits at that time, but Kit had helped him select a new one for the occasion. Slim, looking very dapper in his new suit, he stood by Kit's side while the minister instructed him as to the proper procedure on the morrow.

"Now, Mr. McClintic, when I say, 'Do you take this woman to be your lawfully wedded wife,' you answer, 'I do.'"

"I do," replied McClintic, in a voice which did not seem to belong to him at all.

Kit flashed him one of her quick, broad grins, but he did not smile back. His gray eyes stared at her vacantly as though he had never seen her before. His face, boyish, refined, had a strained look. He ran his hand nervously along the top of his straight, well-brushed, dark hair.

"And finally, Mr. McClintic, you *salute* the bride!" In benign expectancy, the minister beamed.

Guthrie's eyes went blank for a moment, then he lifted his hand to his forehead, turned toward Kit and saluted her as a private salutes his general. "Like this, you mean?" he asked meekly.

"You *kiss* her," answered the minister.

"Oh," replied Guthrie.

The rehearsal over, the two walked out upon the wide porch. "Never mind," laughed Kit. "It's now three-thirty. This time tomorrow it will be all over."

And it was.

The marriage took place at noon. There was Doctor Cornell, Aunt Lydia, looking lovely, her white hair smartly coiffed, gowned in her usual impeccable taste, Kit's uncle and his wife, these were the only witnesses. The groom wore a business suit, the bride wore a simple street frock, and by three o'clock the newlyweds were on their way back to New York and a morning rehearsal.

True to her standard of punctuality, Kit made the rehearsal on time, but the strain of the wedding, the trip back, the natural anxiety as to the rehearsal itself, left her looking pale and tired.

"You look tired, Miss Cornell," Pollock observed.

She told him she had been married only the day before.

He smiled. "In heaven's name, why didn't you tell me? I could easily have let you have a few days more before starting."

Of course, that was something for which Kit would never have asked, but she was grateful to him for his consideration. Pollock put Kit at her ease at once. In a surprisingly short time he was "Allan" and she was "Kit." It did not take her long to ask him the all-important question: "Tell me, Allan, how in the world did you happen to think of me for Sydney?"

"Well," he admitted smilingly, "it was a bit odd. You see, in the boardinghouse where I lived in London were two little old ladies from Scotland. They were artists and the three of us grew very fond of each other. When I decided to bring the show to New York, I sent them to see one of the performances. I valued their opinions and I wanted to see how they would react to the play. They liked

it immensely, and when they came home the three of us
sat for hours talking the whole thing over. I told them, of
course, that in America I intended to play the father myself,
but that I felt that I should have great difficulty in finding
a girl to play Sydney. Then one of them said she remembered an American girl who had played Jo in 'Little
Women.'"

"Good heavens, Allan, that was over two years ago!"

"Yes, I know, but they each remembered your performance and, although they couldn't remember your
name, they were certain that you'd be ideal for Sydney.
After they spoke of you, I recalled seeing you as Jo, and I
agreed with them. The trouble was, I couldn't remember
your name, either, but I got in touch with Leslie Faber
and he told me. So then I sent off the cable and that was all
there was to it."

Fervently, Katharine Cornell blessed the two unknown
Scotch ladies who had played Destiny and given her this
big chance. The more she rehearsed Sydney the more she
loved the part and the more fearful she was of losing it.
Every day Pollock was being told from the Dillingham
office that this Cornell girl was not the type at all, and
anyhow, they asked, who was she? Who had ever heard of
her? Sydney could make or break the play. Then why not
get someone better known for the part? But as yet Pollock
had withstood these arguments.

But knowing that the arguments were taking place did
not make rehearsals easier for Kit. Besides, she was up
against a new director. This man had directed the play in
England, and he kept insisting that she play the part as
the London actress had played it. For Kit, this was difficult

and frightening. Sydney was firmly placed and pictured in her own mind—a Sydney which she felt to be *true*, besides, her intelligence told her that it would be fatal to try to ape the portrayal of another actress.

But the director did not like her and he did all in his power to goad her into giving up the part of her own volition. She was secretly fearful—fearful of many things—of losing the part, of not being able to do it justice, of the sarcasm to which the director constantly subjected her. She writhed under it, she lived under a constant strain, but she hung on.

Working with an unsympathetic director is torture even to the most insensate nature. When she crossed the stage, his voice would snap at her, "*Must* you walk like Henry Irving, Miss Cornell?"—for Irving, despite his greatness, had had a peculiar, awkward walk.

In the evenings she would talk the character of Sydney over with her husband, who approved of her interpretation, a fact which gave her courage as rehearsals became more and more unpleasant.

The terrific strain of rehearsals was augmented by her attempts to get a new apartment in order. The love of home was strong in her, and now that she was married, she was determined to have a real, permanent home of her own. Twenty-three Beekman Place was an old house on the East Side in which she and McClintic had rented three floors.

In 1921 New York's East Side was still a slum. Nobody with any social or professional standing would ever think of living there. But since the last season in Detroit Kit's friendship with the Frank Morgans had continued, and it was Mrs. Morgan who had told her about some of the picturesque old houses on the East Side, and what a splendid view of the East River was to be had from some of them. Looking over the rental ads in the newspaper one Sunday, Kit had seen three floors in a five-story house advertised for rent—cheap. She and Guthrie had taken them. While the place was being made ready, they were living at the Chatham Hotel.

Their friends regarded them in shocked amazement. "Three floors for just the two of you? And on the *East Side?*"

As the time approached closer and closer to the opening, Kit realized that in spite of everything, she was actually going to play Sydney. For her, so much seemed to depend upon this part and this play.

The dress rehearsal was held in Philadelphia where the play was tried out. Then, on October 10, 1921, at the George M. Cohan Theater, came the opening night in New York.

CHARLES DILLINGHAM
presents

A BILL OF DIVORCEMENT

a new play by
Clemence Dane

The mere announcement gives no hint of the hope, the tension, the torrential fear which prevails backstage upon a first night. Actors' eyes as they enter the stage door take on a fevered brightness. In dressing rooms nerves are taut and hands that lift the greasepaint are unsteady. The atmosphere of uncertainty, of strain that borders upon panic pervades everyone connected with the performance. Stage hands feel it. The stage doorman feels it. Telegrams of good wishes, flowers, are arriving momentarily. They remain unseen, unread. Nothing is important at this time, nothing but the play. It might fail. Weeks of work and struggle, months of hope and plans might suddenly be blasted into oblivion. Who knew? The critics will decide all things. The critics will announce to the world whether in their opinion it is a good play or a bad play, and nine times out of ten the world will accept the verdict of the critics.

As is customary after a first performance, people, friends of the actors, friends of the management, crowded back-stage. The audience had been enthusiastic, an enthusiasm which endured among the visitors, who included that night Noel Coward, then a struggling young writer who had been given a seat in the balcony, and Carl van Vechten, the eminent author and music critic. But seasoned professionals have learned not to be misled by this pleasant praise, these exuberant handshakings. While enjoyable, this does not constitute success.

Unfortunately there were four other openings in New York on that night. Only two critics, Charles Darnton and Alan Dale, had chosen to attend "A Bill of Divorcement," while the other critics had attended the other plays. The criticisms of Darnton and Dale were lukewarm and their reviews of Katharine Cornell's portrayal were brief and unpenetrating.

Next morning every member of the cast accepted the stark fact that all hope of success had evaporated. The play had been ignored by most of the critics, and had been given only scant praise by the two who attended. Failure was here, to be recognized and accepted.

Now that all uncertainty was over, Kit began to feel the

prolonged strain under which she had labored during rehearsals. Conflict and confusion had ended. Reaction had
set in. She lost her appetite, and her vitality seemed now
at so low an ebb that she was incapable of taking any interest in anything. The play was going to close—this fine,
worth-while play!

It did not matter that the new apartment was not yet
ready. They had no money with which to do over the place
as they would have liked. They had taken more space than
they needed, more, even, than they could afford to furnish,
because it was very cheap and had a beautiful view. And
now, reading the reviews of Darnton and Dale, Kit did not
care whether the place was ever furnished or not.

Knowing how much the play meant to her and believing
in it wholeheartedly, McClintic shared her disappointment.

"I don't really care—too much—that the critics ignored
me," Kit insisted gamely, "but that the play should flop—
oh, Guthrie, that's unthinkable!"

But they all knew that the play would not, could not
continue when the curtain rang up for the second performance and only two hundred dollars had been taken in at
the box office.

Carl van Vechten, ardent playgoer and play-lover, also
realized that "A Bill of Divorcement" was doomed unless
somebody did something about it. His interest in the play
was purely altruistic. His was simply the appreciation of
the true artist for a fine piece of workmanship. He knew
personally Alexander Woollcott, theatrical critic of the
New York Times. Everybody in New York read Woollcott.

After the second performance when the actors had played
almost to empty seats, van Vechten phoned Woollcott.

"I tell you, it's a wonderful play!" he insisted vehemently. "It's grand stuff, Alec, and unless something's done about it, the thing's going to fold up!"

That was Wednesday morning. Alexander Woollcott made it his business to be present at the Wednesday matinee. Leaving the theater, he, too, felt the injustice of the situation. He wasted no time. Before nightfall he had phoned Heywood Broun and every other critic in New York.

"You've got to see it!" he insisted.

And they did.

Papers the following Sunday printed long, glowing reviews of "A Bill of Divorcement," with the result that by Monday night all seats were sold out and the play became the biggest hit on Broadway.

". . . Katharine Cornell," wrote Woollcott in the Sunday *Times*, "who, as the daughter, has the central and significant role of the play and who therein gives a performance of memorable understanding and beauty . . . Miss Cornell and Mr. Pollock are superb . . ."

All of a sudden Broadway theatergoers became acutely conscious of a new name. Who was this Katharine Cornell? Where did she come from? She was lovely, arresting, different. Here was artistry.

Almost overnight, the entire picture had changed. Success emerged out of failure. Glory took the place of obscurity. And all of Broadway was giving a fervent *Amen* to the message sent by Winthrop Ames to Katharine Cornell:

"I think you're damn swell—my homage to you!"

PART TWO

ATTAINMENT

"THE WAY THINGS HAPPEN"

SEEMINGLY THE young McClintics had suddenly become the darlings of fortune. "A Bill of Divorcement" settled down to a long run, and soon they were occupying their new apartment. McClintic's production of "Dover Road," which opened in December, 1921, had brought success to him simultaneously with the success of his wife. Both, however, were looking ahead to even higher achievements, for the desire for perfection in their vocation was ever the driving force of their existence. Meanwhile, they were adjusting themselves to each other and to their new life. Kit admitted frankly that Guthrie, eternally young, inspired her. She was happy, happier now than she had ever dreamed of being, happy in her home, happy in the part she was playing in the theater, in her friends, and particularly in her husband.

In March, 1922, the Beekman Place house was offered for sale and Guthrie bought it with the money he had made on "Dover Road." After buying the place, they let the former owners rent from them, and continued to live on the top floors.

The coming of summer, which meant the end of the theatrical season, brought the closing of both "A Bill of

Divorcement" and "Dover Road," and the McClintics went blithely off to Europe on the *SS. Scandinavian,* Kit having already signed a contract to play Mary Fitton in "Will Shakespeare," a play which Winthrop Ames was to produce at the National Theater the first of the year.

No wider variance of characterization could have been presented to any actress than the parts of Sydney and Mary Fitton. Sydney was sensitive, emotional, lovable, pathetic; Mary was bold and bawdry, passionate and stormy. During the run of "A Bill of Divorcement" several parts had been offered Kit, but she was now in a position to choose the sort of part she wanted to play, and she had chosen Mary because, while it was not long, it was colorful and it was a splendid opportunity to prove her versatility.

Barely a year ago she had gone from office to office, rarely being admitted within the little fence, rarely interviewing anyone higher than office boys and telephone girls. Those days were now in the past. Managers sought her services. Al Woods, who was something of a power on Broadway, offered to star her. Kit liked Woods—everybody on Broadway liked him—a tall, dark, heavily set, jovial and full-spirited man, who produced over four hundred plays during his career, and called every man and woman in his many companies "sweetheart."

But while liking Woods and appreciating his knowledge of the theater, Katharine Cornell felt that she was not yet ready for stardom, felt that she must do even harder work before she had earned the right to it. To her, stardom meant more than merely her name flashing in electric bulbs over the marquee of a theater. When it came for her it must be no flimsy, evanescent thing. It must be built firmly on long endeavor and it must evolve naturally out of rigid adherence to her own highest ideal. She had seen stardom come to others, seen it come too soon, and in consequence seen it last a year, two years, possibly five—and then oblivion.

Often she had asked herself why the careers of many modern stars were of such brief duration, and invariably she reached the conclusion that it was not because of the fickleness of the public taste, but because stardom had not been honestly earned. Actually, the careers of those actors who had built solidly had been lengthy. Garrick acted for thirty years. Irving's career on the stage covered forty-nine years. Edwin Booth's career lasted forty-four years, while forty years encompassed the theatrical activities of his father. The career of Mrs. Siddons lasted about fifty years. Macready's endured forty years, and Charles Kean's, forty-two. Lawrence Barrett's stage activities lasted thirty-eight years. Betterton, who preceded Garrick, had a career which covered fifty years. Joseph Jefferson's career was longer than any of them. The beloved Jo Jefferson had begun acting as a child, had even been carried on the stage as a baby, and had continued until one year before his death at seventy-six in 1905. These truly great ones proved that a career in the theater is not necessarily a transient and precarious thing, a thing dependent upon youth. They had proven that the public which, after all, decides such matters, is intensely loyal when it is convinced of genuine merit.

Katharine Cornell could wait for her reward. She was now twenty-four. Behind her lay six years of almost unceasing work, but when the opportunity for stardom was offered, she refused it because, as she said simply, she "had not worked hard enough or long enough."

Despite the fact that "Will Shakespeare" had a brilliant cast, it ran for only twelve weeks, and Kit began rehearsals for "The Enchanted Cottage" which William Brady, Jr., was producing and which the redoubtable Jessie Bonstelle was directing.

Again Katharine Cornell was seen in a sharply differing character than that of the tempestuous and beautiful Mary Fitton, for Laura Pennington in "The Enchanted Cottage" was an ethereal creature, frail and wistful. The play opened on March 31, 1923, and it suffered the same lamentable fate as had "Will Shakespeare."

The finances of the McClintics were now decidedly low. It was neither pleasant nor promising for an actress, having made an outstanding initial success, to follow it with two plays which could be classed under the heading of failure. Like his wife, McClintic was also learning what it was to face "the slings and arrows of outrageous fortune." No longer with the Ames office, he was now an independent producer. This meant that he was responsible for the costs of the plays which he presented, responsible for all production expenses including the salaries of his actors.

"Dover Road" had made money, part of which he had used to buy their house, and the rest of which he now proceeded to lose on his next two productions, "Gringo" and "A Square Peg."

With the thoroughness with which she would have tackled a new part, Kit bravely took over the housework. But though she was an excellent cook and actually enjoyed cooking, she had no desire to continue these labors indefinitely.

It was at this time that Gilbert Miller sent for her to discuss the part of Henriette in "Casanova," a new play which he planned to present at the Empire Theater in September.

But like the two preceding it, this play was not a real success.

At twenty-five Katharine Cornell was a radiantly attractive woman. Her face, with its heavily lidded eyes, beautifully chiseled nose and finely arched brows, had taken on a greater strength, had achieved a symmetry which had not been noticeable in girlhood. Her body, slender, patrician, statuesque, had taken on a firm and delicate roundness. Being tall and lithe, she wore the new tailleurs, the skirts of which now reached just above the ankles, to particular advantage. People were saying that she was beautiful, but no one could ever get her to believe it. Even then, she hated discussing herself. Her friends could bring up any current subject and she would discuss it freely, even at times brilliantly, but let them introduce the subject of Katharine Cornell and she shied away from it like a skittish horse at a flying newspaper. Meeting her, she gave one a sense of complete repose. Her manner was completely devoid of tension.

When "Casanova" closed, McClintic was reading a new play by Clemence Dane, who had authored "A Bill of Divorcement" and "Will Shakespeare," called "The Way Things Happen." He believed in it, and his faith was shared by his wife. Why should they not do this play together? Both were firmly convinced that here at last, after so many failures, was the play they wanted. McClintic would direct and produce it, while Kit would play Shirley Pride, the lead. Hours upon hours they sat before the fireplace talking of the play, discussing costumes, the set, the cast. 1923 had been a bleak and difficult year for both of them, but now surely—ah, *surely*—

"The Way Things Happen" opened in Philadelphia, where it played for three weeks. Philadelphia cheered it, crowded the theater to see it, and hopes were high when the curtain went up at the Lyceum Theater in New York on January 28, 1924.

When the curtain came down that night and the Mc-Clintics returned to Beekman Place, they faced the unpleasant fact that they had spent their money, their time, their hopes on another failure.

One took these things as quietly as possible and tried not to feel too badly about it. Every play is, after all, a gamble. In show business one must learn to accept the bad with the good, and keep hoping. They had gambled and they had lost.

"The Way Things Happen" had only a three weeks' run, and during this time the offer came to Kit to play Lalage Sturges in "The Outsider," which was already being tried out in other cities and was soon to be brought to New York. But she hesitated.

"No," she said, "I'd have to take the place of the girl who is being discharged. I hate doing that."

"But," pleaded the manager, "I'll have to let her go, anyway. If you don't take the part, I'll simply have to get someone else."

"We-ell, in that case—"

"Now," he suggested, "why don't you run up to Baltimore and catch the show and see what you think of the part?"

"All right, I'll go to Baltimore and look the show over, but I won't take the part unless I'm sure I can play it."

With the closing of their own play, Kit and her husband immediately took the train for Baltimore, uppermost in their minds the question, would she or would she not play Lalage? The part was that of a crippled girl, and almost from the first scene Kit knew that this part was meant for her.

"I can do Lalage," she told her husband, when they were talking it over after the performance.

"Sure, you can. It's your part, Kit."

"Yes, but, you know, Guthrie, it seems to me that the trouble is that that part hasn't been rightly directed. I mean —well, you take a girl crippled like that, the director has made her walk all over the stage as often as possible. That's wrong. She'd be too sensitive about her condition. She'd walk just as little as possible, don't you see? She's hungry for love, and she believes that no man will fall in love with her because she's a cripple. Well, it seems to me if I were that girl, I'd walk just as little as I possibly *could!*"

"You're right, Kit. A girl like that would do as little walking as possible."

"Then I'll sign the contract only if I feel that the director will agree to let me play Lalage as I think she should be played."

The contract was signed and work begun, work which crowded to capacity each night as well as each day, for the play was to open in New York City in less than a week. It was a week of incessant study, incessant rehearsing. Finally, on Sunday night in New York came the dress rehearsal. It continued for hours, beginning during the mid-afternoon and ending shortly before dawn. The producer, William Harris, Jr., insisted that the last act was wrong. Author, director, even the actors, all tried frantically to change it. They tried it this way, they tried it that way. They put in lines and took them out. They deleted "business" only to replace it. And, at long last, everyone jadedly agreed that the original version was best, after all.

"Okay, folks, okay," called the director wearily, "we'll leave it as is. Come on, now, come on. I know you're tired, but—let's take the last act right from the beginning again!"

When McClintic called for his wife at the 49th Street Theater while the rehearsal was in progress, he found her pale, nerve-torn, almost at the point of collapse. He watched her worriedly. She had not slept for the past week—and tomorrow night was the opening performance. Looking at her now, he asked himself, would Kit be able to play at all?

But the next night she gave one of the most inspired performances of her life. "Katharine Cornell," wrote Arthur Hornblow in the *Theater Magazine*, "again covers herself with glory . . ."

"The Outsider" was a hit. People were buying seats weeks in advance. Seemingly the play would run indefinitely; and then, after thirteen weeks came the actors' strike and "The Outsider," in common with nine other Broadway shows, was compelled to close. To this day each of the actors who went out on strike at that time carries a gold star on their Equity cards. The star indicates that an actor was not idle at the time of the strike, that he was an Equity member in good standing and that he actually left employment in order to uphold a principle. His gold star indicates that he made a sacrifice at that time.

Equity is the name of the actors' union which was organized in May, 1913, with Francis Wilson as its first president. At the time of its organization many actors had hotly refused to join, arguing that a union would lower their dignity, take them out of the ranks of artists and place them on a par with day-laborers. What, they demanded, was the profession coming to?

In the old days conditions among actors had been deplorable. If business failed to come in, salaries often failed to be forthcoming. A manager could leave a company stranded anywhere and there was nothing the actor could do about it. Actors were required to pay their own transportation to the place of opening and from the place of closing. Salaries were small and without regulation. Rehearsals could drag on for months without payment. A manager could and often did dismiss an actor on a week's notice.

The first meeting of the Actors' Equity Association had been attended by one hundred and twelve daring souls determined upon the protective measure of an actors' union. The managers heard about it—and laughed. What? Actors thinking they could dictate terms? Absurd. Ridiculous.

By 1919 Equity could boast of over three thousand members, among them some of the biggest names in the business. The managers were not laughing now. They were bitterly determined upon Equity's downfall. Let an actor hold out for an Equity contract—just let him try, that was all. He would never get any work, not with any manager in show business. He'd be blacklisted as long as he lived.

That year, 1919, had been the most momentous year in the history of the theater. It was the year of the actors' strike, and it was the year that Equity affiliated with the American Federation of Labor.

The strike was won by the actors. Equity had achieved much. It had won a fair contract, but it had not as yet been able to enforce the closed shop. This now, in the spring of 1924, was the main issue.

McClintic knew that it would all adjust itself satisfactorily, and meanwhile—"It's June," he remarked, with a tinge of wistfulness in his pleasantly modulated voice.

Knowing that this was not the idle statement that it seemed, Kit waited expectantly.

"It would be a good time to take a holiday abroad," he suggested, after a slight pause.

"*Let's!*" said Kit.

So they left the strike behind them and went roaming over the highways of the Old World.

The strike had been settled when they returned in early fall. Scarcely had Kit landed in New York before David Belasco sent for her. Belasco, affectionately called "the old master," was seventy-one now. He was a short man with a strong, unlined face and a shock of white hair. He always put his collar on backward, like a priest. His theatrical activities had covered a wide range. Beginning as a call-boy in a San Francisco theater, he had been an actor, he had directed stock in Salt Lake City in the company in which Maude Adams had played as a child; he had written plays, he had turned producer, and he had built his own theater. In the old days actors, approaching Belasco for a job, saw him sitting in a swivel chair before a battered desk. But now his offices above the Belasco Theater were furnished in a rich, pseudo-monastic style—high-backed carved chairs with red plush seats; heavy, deeply carved tables; stained glass windows; candlesticks and thick carpets; a Louis XVI chaise longue and the smell of joss sticks; chimes instead of buzzers to summon his assistants; the office dimly lighted, and in the midst of it all, Belasco—with his desk on a Ming dais. Here he reigned like a monarch. For forty-five years he had been connected with the theater and many of the greatest stage figures of the day owed their success to this white-haired, kindly man: Mrs. Leslie Carter, David Warfield, E. H. Sothern, Blanche Bates, Lenore Ulric, Frances Starr.

On a brisk autumnal day in 1924, amidst his churchlike surroundings which looked more like a stage set than anything he presented in the theater, Belasco talked to Kit about a new play he intended to produce called "Tiger Cats," in which he offered her the lead, the part of Susanne Chaumont.

Kit did not decide at once. In her opinion it was a thoroughly unpleasant play and the part of Susanne was an unsympathetic, detestable character. She talked the matter over with Guthrie.

"But," he asked, "if you don't like the part, why do you even consider playing it?"

The answer was characteristic of Katharine Cornell. "Because, don't you see? It's just because I *don't* like it, that I think I ought to play it! *It will be such excellent discipline!*"

That she, now twenty-six and having been on the stage

for eight years, should have accepted a part merely because she considered it discipline proved the sincerity of her determination to build her career on a solid foundation.

Having made her decision and commenced the study of the part, she conceived within her own mind a clear-cut idea as to how this difficult character of Susanne should be played. Susanne was an utterly selfish, insensate, heartless, domineering wife who, through vanity, lack of appreciation and the desire to dominate him, finally succeeds in ruining her husband's career. The part could be played in two ways, either noisily or quietly. The play had already been produced in London, and the capable actress who had played the part there, had chosen the former way, with the result that the author, director and leading man could not conceive of Susanne being played in any other manner.

Kit, having intelligently analyzed the character, felt that she could not play the part noisily or stridently and decided that it could be given an even greater force by the quiet interpretation. In the face of concerted opposition from author, director, and the leading man, Robert Loraine, she valiantly adhered to her principles. Rehearsals became a long series of bickerings—the three men against the one woman. Harassed, yet standing firmly for what she believed to be right, Kit spent wakeful, wretched nights. Rehearsals were something to be dreaded. Belasco, still vigorous and still a powerful figure in his own little world, paced back and forth exclaiming, "No, no, you mustn't bother Miss Katharine like this! I won't have you bother Miss Katharine!"

"But, governor—" the director would expostulate, and a lengthy harangue would follow.

Everybody was distressed, everybody was fidgety. Usually

an atmosphere of camaraderie prevails at rehearsals, but anyone drifting into the Belasco Theater and watching the rehearsals then in progress, would have come away with the conviction that "Tiger Cats" had been appropriately named.

There was a scene in which Loraine, as the husband, fires a pistol. To make matters worse, during one of the rehearsals, he held the revolver too close to Kit's arm. Though it contained only a blank cartridge, its explosion at so close a range caused a painful burn. The arm became inflamed. Day and night it ached from her hand to her shoulder, and almost hysterical now with the strain of the whole thing, Katharine Cornell prayed.

"Oh, God," she begged wildly, "let me get blood poisoning! Let them have to cut off my arm! Let anything happen —*anything*—just so I won't have to go on with this awful part!"

But a benign Providence had no ears to hear such a supplication. The arm healed. The director stormed. The author moaned. The producer paced back and forth. The leading man buried his head in his hands.

In spite of all this, "Tiger Cats" opened at the Belasco Theater on October 21, 1924. Katharine Cornell received an excellent press, but even though fortified with the immense prestige of the old master, Belasco, the play itself was not a hit. It settled down for a run, however, and gradually the fermentation of rehearsals came to seem like some utterly fantastic dream.

During the actors' strike, while the actors were striving to achieve stipulated concessions from the managers, Francis Wilson had founded an organization called the Actor's Theater. Wilson himself was a top-ranking star. In his younger days he had worked with that grand old actor, Jo Jefferson, and his love for acting was as great as was that of Jefferson himself. Here was a beautiful and lofty ideal— an actual actor's theater, run by actors, where actors could play their favorite plays for matinees, where the great actors of the day were each to play for two weeks receiving no remuneration whatever, merely to play the parts they loved for the sheer delight of playing them. Thus, while appearing in a hit play at a New York theater, a star would appear simultaneously for matinees at the Actor's Theater.

Guthrie McClintic had been given full charge and was to remain in charge for the next two years, during which time he was also engaged in producing other plays at other theaters. Splendid though Wilson's idea was, it at length proved impractical, for the stars, working at parts which required their utmost in strength and freshness, found it unwise further to tax themselves by appearing at the same time for matinees in another theater.

But in the beginning and now in 1924, it looked as if the Actor's Theater were firmly established. The play under consideration at this time was George Bernard Shaw's "Candida." Who, asked the founders, would they invite to play the title role? It did not necessarily have to be a star, but it did have to be someone with a following, an actress of consummate artistry.

Kit was frankly thrilled and delighted when she learned that she, of all the actresses then in New York, had been chosen for this much-coveted role. "Candida" was one of her favorite parts.

Even though she was playing a trying role each night and though she was to receive no payment, she entered zestfully into the study of that charming character, Candida.

A current resentment and jealousy ran through Broadway as players asked each other: "Why should *she* be chosen? Why should such a part be given to Cornell? She isn't a star!"

On the afternoon of "Candida's" opening, McClintic was rehearsing "Mrs. Partridge Presents" at another theater. This, to him, was torture. Minute by minute he kept asking himself how was the play going? Was Kit well received? Would the Broadway prejudice somehow affect her performance? She had promised to come to his rehearsal the minute "Candida" was over, and he kept watching for her anxiously.

When finally she walked in, he rushed toward her. "How were you?" he asked excitedly.

"Oh," she answered, "I was all right, I suppose."

"All right!" he exclaimed. "All right! Candida *can't* be all right! She must be either magnificent or—*terrible!*"

Impatiently he awaited the criticisms which told him next day that Katharine Cornell as Candida *had* been magnificent. In fact, "Candida" was such a success that when "Tiger Cats" closed, it was put on an eight-performance weekly basis.

But great as this triumph was, there was an even greater one to follow.

CHAPTER ELEVEN

STARDOM

By 1925 THERE were few grownups in England and America who had not read Michael Arlen's novel, "The Green Hat." It was the day of the flapper. The flapper was a girl whose figure was hipless, flat-chested, boyish; whose galoshes, perpetually open, flapped as she walked; whose hair was cut close to her head, shingled in the back almost like a man's; whose skirts were at the knee or slightly above it; whose hat was a small, closely fitting felt; and who smoked cigarettes from a long holder—the longer the smarter. It was an age which boasted of its sophistication. It was a time when conversation inevitably turned to Freud, prohibition, Doug Fairbanks, Mary Pickford, Charles Chaplin, Michael Arlen—and "The Green Hat."

During their European vacation the previous year, the McClintics had read the book. Guthrie called it "claptrap," but Kit said that if it were ever dramatized she would like to play Iris March, the heroine.

It was during the production of "Candida" that Al Woods approached McClintic to direct the dramatization of the best seller, and after first considering Jeanne Eagles for the part of Iris, offered it to Kit. The play would have its out-of-town tryout in Detroit and Chicago, and would come to the Broadhurst Theater in New York on September 15, 1925.

Like every other part Kit had played, Iris became a picture in her mind. She then proceeded to externalize that picture, to make others see what she saw, see it sharply, vividly. Before it is given to the public, a character in a play emerges through several channels. It is first a thought-picture in the mind of the author. It is the business of the actress to take that picture into her *own* consciousness, analyze it, understand it, distinctly visualize it, and then convincingly portray it.

Each character has its own peculiarities—its own way of walking, talking, smiling, sitting, standing, gesturing. Much contemplation must precede the actual rendition. The audience views a finished, well-rounded product, little realizing the thought that has gone before. To be successful the actress must make the audience forget that it is seeing a play, forget that it is seeing Katharine Cornell and see only the being called Iris March. It must sympathize with her, love her, laugh with her, but most of all it must *feel* with her.

So it was with every part Katharine Cornell played. Every part required hours of activity and hours of seeming inactivity; hours of sitting quietly before the fireplace apparently doing nothing, yet gradually becoming acquainted with a new person who may be called Iris March or Mary Fitton or Henriette or Lalage Sturges. It is a curious thing, something comprehensible only to the actor—how a character dominates the actor and yet at the same time the actor dominates the character. To the actor the character becomes a living creature from whom he cannot escape for long. It is as if the character comes to live *in* and *with* the actor, so that the actor is always thinking about it; and yet it is the intelligence of the actor which decrees how the character is going to do a certain thing in a certain scene.

Katharine Cornell explains it this way: "You want to do a certain thing in a certain scene. You've thought about it, worked it all out using imagination and the best ability you have. Then comes the performance—and you do that which you have planned to do. You do it sincerely and as well as you can. And at that moment nothing else in all the world matters. It doesn't even matter whether or not the audience will like it. Later—yes; later. Then you can think back to the audience; but not *then*. To act, thinking only of the audience, spoils your performance."

Sitting before the fireplace now, she knew that everybody who would see the play had read the book, and each person would have already formed his conception of Iris March. Her problem, therefore, was all the more difficult because physically she did not in the least resemble the Iris March whom Michael Arlen had created. The author's description of Iris was that of someone small and with red hair, while Katharine Cornell was tall and had dark hair. Despite this, Kit had no doubt of her ability to play Iris. She felt that she understood Iris even better than she had understood Henriette and some of the other parts she had played.

McClintic frankly disliked the play as much as he had the book. When Woods approached him to direct the production he had at first refused.

"I don't like it," he insisted. "It's artificial. Kit, you're crazy to play that part!"

But Kit was firm, and he was finally persuaded to undertake the direction. Rehearsals began during the run of "Candida."

In the production of a play for Broadway, effects are sometimes achieved inspirationally. During rehearsals an actor will often unintentionally make some telling move, will even interpolate a line at which the director may exclaim delightedly, "That's good! That's good! We'll leave it in!" But these happy occasions are rare. Effects are usually achieved painstakingly. The slight droop of a hand, a sudden turn, the raising of an eyebrow, the slowness or quickness of a smile—even such little things as these are tried again and again, now one way, now another. Usually even the lifting of a teacup is timed, as is the very quickness or slowness with which an actor responds to his cue. Every pause becomes significant and important, every glance carries its message. Watching all this during a performance, the audience thinks: "Ah! How *natural* that is! How *spontaneously* she did that!" Yet untold patience has gone into every minute action. Hours might be spent upon a simple gesture which requires only a moment or two in its execution.

Guthrie McClintic was admitted to be one of the most gifted and inspired directors of the modern theater. There are directors who achieve their effects by swearing, pacing back and forth, ranting, whipping their actors with sarcasm. But McClintic's direction was poised, kindly, quiet. Wearing a sleeveless white sweater and smoking almost incessantly, he sat at the left of the table close to the footlights. His directions were given calmly. His rehearsals were conducted with thoroughness and dignity. He had acquired the knack of getting the best out of his actors by encouraging them, trying to see things from their point of view, yet always maintaining a firm, sure hand.

Now and then instead of giving orders, he acted out a scene while the player stood aside watching. Sometimes the actor would say apologetically, "But I—I just don't *feel* it that way, Mr. McClintic."

McClintic might have stormed about and declared vehemently that it must be done the way he wanted it or not at all, but such uncouth tactics were not his way.

"All right," he answered quietly, "all right, let's see how you feel it."

Watching her husband conduct a rehearsal, Katharine Cornell always felt a great pride in him. To her there was no finer director in show business than Guthrie McClintic; while to McClintic the stage had no finer actress than Katharine Cornell.

"Kit embodies and projects beauty," he declared. "She can be young or old, radiant or dull, splendid, drab, inspired, buoyant, harsh, grief-stricken—whatever she chooses to be."

Though they had been married now for four years, their mutual love of the theater had drawn them closer and closer together. Sometimes she thought of the art of acting as being akin to painting. It was not enough, she knew, for an actor to feel an emotion, he must be able to project that emotion so that his audience shared it. Her years on the stage had taught her not only to feel the emotion, but to be master of it, to temper or to intensify it at will.

Finally came the opening night in Detroit. The Garrick Theater was crowded. In her dressing room, Kit was battling that old, old enemy—stagefright. Always before a performance that singular dread would come over her, something stark and horrible, which required all her strength to control.

Eveline, her maid, who had been with her for three years now, watched her concernedly. Rarely did Kit talk much before a performance, feeling that she must save her voice and her energy for the role she was playing, but stagefright has the effect of making one even more silent. Eveline was well conversant with the signs of stagefright. Eveline was wise and tactful, quiet, stately, efficient. Thin, with very white teeth, beautifully regular features and a dark skin, she hailed from Jamaica and was proud of being a British subject. Knowing the torture Kit was going through, and knowing her own inability to mitigate it, Eveline kept thinking that she wished this night were over.

"You have nothing to worry about, Miss Cornell," she murmured gently.

Kit did not answer.

"Overture!" came the call of the stage manager. "First act, everybody! Places!"

There was a short, electric pause. Then, in a hushed voice, as if she were speaking to herself, Eveline said: "Curtain—going—up!"

Curtain going up; the three magic words which invariably brought a kind of awe and an increased tension. This was the big moment—this would always be the big moment in Katharine Cornell's life.

And finally, inevitably, the curtain was coming down. There were curtain calls, there was enthusiastic applause, and next day there were the glowing praises of the Detroit critics. Woods was pleased. McClintic was pleased, Eveline was pleased. Leslie Howard, playing the male lead, and Ann Harding, playing Venice, were pleased. But—would New York be pleased? After all, that alone mattered. They all felt that they had a hit but, being wise in show business, they awaited anxiously the verdict of the metropolis.

But New York accepted "The Green Hat" with open arms and an open heart. The play ran twenty-nine weeks in Manhattan alone, but Katharine Cornell played Iris for over two years, for Woods sent the play on tour to the larger cities. Wrote George Jean Nathan in the *Morning Telegraph*, ". . . It is superbly acted in its leading role by that one young woman who stands head and shoulders above all other young women of the American theater, Miss Katharine Cornell."

In Buffalo, while playing "The Green Hat," the young woman who, according to the eminent Mr. Nathan, stood head and shoulders above every other young woman of the American theater, was called upon for a speech at the end of the performance.

"Speech!" shouted the audience. "Cornell! Speech!"

Backstage, people crowded about her, everyone talking at once.

"Speech! They want a speech!"

"You'll have to make a speech!"

Katharine Cornell found herself walking on the stage. The applause subsided. There was a hush, pulsing, abysmal.

"For years," began the leading lady bravely enough, "for years I have planned what I would say if ever I were called upon to make a speech—" she stopped, gazed helplessly at the audience, bowed—and walked off the stage!

When "The Green Hat" was produced in New York,

Katharine Cornell was not yet a star. She still believed that
the star system was wrong and, essentially modest, she still
felt that she was not yet ready for stardom; but even now
it was as if stardom were playing with her that old childish
game, and singing out: "Ready or not, here I come!"

She had been on the stage now almost ten years. Back
in 1916 when he learned that his daughter was seeking
work with the Washington Square Players, "Doc" Cornell
had said, "Oh, she's just a stagestruck kid!" It was true.
She was just a stagestruck kid. Now she was no longer a
kid. She was twenty-seven. Behind her were years of enterprise and hardship—yet she was still stagestruck. Never had
she lost the capacity for being thrilled by the theater.
Never once had she regretted the dominant motive which
had forced her to become an actress.

There was an afternoon rehearsal in Brooklyn that day.
As Kit and Guthrie were leaving the theater, the electrician
grinned at them.

"Say, Miss Cornell, when yuh come back to th' theater
t'night, better look up at th' front of th' house."

"Why?"

"We-ell, I ain't sayin'. All I know is, I got my orders.
Th' lights're gonna be changed out front t'night. Better
just give 'um th' once over b'fore yuh start makin' up."

"What do you suppose he means, Guthrie?" she asked,
when the two were outside.

McClintic smiled boyishly. "It could mean only one
thing, Kit. Woods has been talking about starring you for
a long time."

"I know, but—but—"

"And, of course, he doesn't want the Brooklyn audiences

or the audiences on the road to think that this isn't the original New York cast."

They walked for several blocks in silence, each engrossed in his own thoughts.

"Well, Kit," said McClintic, "it's here. Stardom. It's here. You've earned it. It belongs to you."

She did not answer. Suppose that *had* been what the electrician meant? How would she feel a few hours from now if she should look up and see her own name in lights over the front of the theater? What would it mean to her? Tribute? Glory? Elation? In reality, she told herself, it would only mean one thing—*responsibility.* She glanced at her husband. He was frankly excited, happy. But she? She could not seem to feel anything.

"If it's really so," she told herself, "I suppose I'll only *feel* when I actually *see* it. That will be the kind of moment one reads about."

But when, several hours later, they gazed upward at the lights over the theater, it amazed her that she still did not *feel.*

As there had not been enough room for the whole name, the lights above the marquee read:

KATH CORNELL

IN

THE GREEN HAT

She realized that, oddly enough, this was a bigger moment for her husband than for herself. She had expected the moment to be shimmering, beautiful, electric. She had expected to feel deeply; feel joy—tears—excitement—pride. But now she did not feel anything except *humility.*

Standing there so quietly beside her husband, Katharine
Cornell realized that stardom would bring its own burdens.
Being a star meant increased responsibilities—responsibility
not alone to one's fellow-actors, but for the entire performance. A leading woman has an understudy, a star has
none. The illness of the leading woman means that the play
can still go on, but to be a star means to be billed above
the play, and an indisposed star necessitates the closing of
the show. Too, while a leading lady might deplore ineffi-
cient stage management, she would consider any lapses
in that department none of her business. For her to take
the stage manager to task would be presumption; while
should the lights not function promptly on cue, should the
curtain be too slow or too quick in descending, the star
must make it her business to find out *why*.

Intelligently, without heroics, without self-glorification,
Katharine Cornell accepted stardom that night, never for
an instant shrinking from the responsibility which the honor
entailed.

CHAPTER TWELVE

GERTRUDE MACY

*B*EFORE THE run of "The Green Hat" reached its conclusion, Kit was already studying another play. She did not like the Somerset Maugham drama, "The Letter," and said so. However, she stood alone in her opinion. Everyone else thought the play was wonderful.

All this time, watching Kit's career with more than friendly interest, were two men who were later to further it in a concrete way. One was Conger Goodyear, who had known Kit back in her wire-walking days; the other was Stanton Griffis. Both were ardent theater-goers, both had implicit faith in the genius of Katharine Cornell.

"Why," they were asking McClintic now, "don't you and Kit manage your own productions?"

The two men were ready, they affirmed, to invest their money in such an enterprise. Why shouldn't Katharine Cornell be her own manager? Guthrie and Kit talked it over lengthily, liking the idea. Instead of "Katharine Cornell in . . ." it would be "Katharine Cornell presents . . ."

Yes, they liked the idea, but this, they agreed, was not the time. Someday, some fine future day it would happen, but not now. If such a company were ever formed, it must

148

be the sort of organization wherein Kit and he would be able to produce whatever play they chose without being harassed by having to keep an eye on "box office." To this the two men readily agreed. It would not be primarily a money-making venture for any of them.

Kit, herself, declared that if such a thing ever happened, even though she were a manager she would work on a salary, so that anything above this stipulated sum could be put back into the finances of the company as an insurance against possible future losses. She knew that producing plays must always be a gamble; besides, by holding herself to a definite salary, she was removing the profit motive from her activities, lifting them above mere commercialism. The more she thought of Goodyear's and Griffis' proposal, the more she realized what it would mean to her. It was all something hazy as yet, something to which one might look forward, something glorious which, however, might not materialize.

The idea was not new. Many great actors have desired to be their own managers and thus liberate themselves from the taboos of commercialism. Garrick had been an actor-manager. Macready, Phelps, John Philip Kemble and Charles Kemble were all actor-managers. Booth had put every dollar he earned into the building of his own theater, went into debt and finally into bankruptcy through his lofty desire to give to the American public all that was best. Irving, more fortunate, took over the Lyceum Theater in London, managing, producing, acting, and made millions despite the fact that he put art first and "box office" second. This same ideal now animated Katharine Cornell and Guthrie McClintic. When the time came, they were ready

to risk all they had in order to produce in freedom that
which they considered worthy.

But now there was "The Letter" which made a phe-
nomenal success. For an hour after the ringing down of the
final curtain hordes of people gathered outside the stage
entrance of the Morosco Theater. They made a respectful
little aisle as Katharine Cornell, plainly dressed, a scarf
knotted trimly about her throat, a small felt hat smartly
tilted, walked to her car. At sight of her, hundreds of voices
rose in a spontaneous cheer. Those who were there that
night said she kept her head very low, and those who were
close enough to get a good look at her declared that there
were tears of gratitude in her eyes.

After a run of thirteen weeks in New York "The Letter"
went on tour, closing in September, 1927. The McClintics
went to Santa Barbara for a rest. Here, stretched at ease in
the California sun, Kit thought soberly about the future.
There is an old Chinese proverb which declares that "Every
man must enter into the garden of his soul, alone." This,
now, she was seeking to do. She knew that for the most
part theatrical managers were purely businessmen, entering
show business because they hoped to make money out of
it. The manager creates a star, not because he considers the
person merits it, but primarily because he hopes to profit
financially. Katharine Cornell was too well balanced, too
sensible, not to know the value of money, but she was also
too wise in the ways of the theater to permit her talent to
be commercialized. She had not become an actress because she either needed or wanted money. She had become
an actress simply because she could not imagine herself
ever being anything else. There was one thing she deter-

mined upon, and that was never to permit herself to become a "type" actress, an actress who plays only one kind of part. As usual, her husband was in complete accord with her aspiration.

There was another person to whom she talked, who also understood her and appreciated all that she was standing for—that was Gertrude Macy.

The two had met briefly long years ago, but it was during those quiet days in Santa Barbara that they met again and made the discovery that they were kindred spirits.

Kit had bought the dramatization of "The Age of Innocence" which was to be her next production, and which Gilbert Miller wanted to present and finance. Both she and McClintic were enthusiastic about it, an enthusiasm which now Gertrude Macy came to share.

The action of the play was laid in the seventies, at the time when Worth was the world's most fashionable modiste. Since Gilbert Miller had agreed to have Kit's clothes made by Worth, she was planning to leave at once for Paris. McClintic was unable to accompany her, and lolling at ease in his beach chair, he looked meditatively at Gertrude Macy.

Little did Gert know then of the change this meeting was about to make in her life. At school she had never been even slightly interested in dramatics. She had majored in math and physics. Riding, polo, these to her were more exciting than all the plays in the world. Her family were Californians, always spending their summers in Santa Barbara, and now she was simply making a neighborly call upon two people whom she honestly liked and whom she had met on shipboard while going to Europe some years

before. It did not matter at all to Gert that Guthrie and
Kit were connected with the theater or that they were
famous. She liked them as *people*. She liked them because
they were unassuming, because they were wholly without
airs, because of their innate refinement and intelligence,
because they were *genuine*.

There was no nonsense about Gertrude, nothing either
fluffy or flighty. She was a forthright person, active, vital,
as alert as a terrier. Five feet eight inches tall, a little
younger than Kit, she was largely boned and slender. Behind horn-rimmed glasses, her eyes were bright, candid,
unwavering. She had a clear, healthy-looking skin, and if
she used any make-up it was not discernible. Her teeth
were white and strong, and when she smiled McClintic realized it was because she felt like it, not because it was
expected of her. Her dark hair was short—clean-looking,
crisp, shiny hair which waved naturally. No fussy hair-dos
for Gertrude. She had no time for such things. She ran a
comb quickly through it, and her hair was dressed. She
had a firm, free, confident stride, and went in for low·
heeled oxfords, plain, well-tailored suits, hats that could
be yanked on without a mirror. Her sense of humor, while
not obtrusive, was unfailing. Her poise was unshakable.
There was calmness in her—deep, strong, inherent. One
felt upon meeting her that she was practical and patient,
sympathetic and co-operative, dependable and loyal. One
could no more question the integrity, stability and intelligence of Gertrude Macy than one could question the
shining of the sun. McClintic liked her, trusted her, and
it was obvious that Kit liked her.

He realized that she knew nothing about theatrical business and that she was quite content *not* to know anything about it, but—

"Look here," he said suddenly, breaking in upon the two women as they discussed costumes, "why don't you go along to Paris and take care of Kit?"

There was a brief moment of silence. "I mean it," he went on in his quiet, amiable way. "You see, I'll be tied up in New York. I can't possibly get away at this time. And I've been hating the thought of Kit crossing alone. Why don't you go along and look after her?"

Gertrude Macy was a shockproof individual. If the offer came as a surprise, she gave no indication of it. Before she could answer, Kit, leaning toward her eagerly, asked, "Why not? Yes, come along!"

Gertrude Macy could see no reason in the world why not, so in her straightforward, down-to-earth way, she grinned and answered, "All right."

This association commenced with Gertrude assuming the official position of secretary, although she was friend, adviser, stand-by, confidante and buffer as well. If anything went wrong, it was Gertrude who calmly, without any fuss, fixed it. Quietly, efficiently, she took charge of all Katharine Cornell's affairs, and eventually became Kit's manager.

"Gert," according to Katharine Cornell, "runs the whole shooting match." Paris was no stranger to her. Having spent three years at Bryn Mawr College, she had already been abroad several times, and had once achieved the seemingly impossible by traveling throughout Europe without a passport. Yes, as McClintic had surmised that sunny afternoon in Santa Barbara, she was just the person to "look after Kit."

The clothes they bought in Paris for the part of Ellen Olenska filled them both with delight. Being tall and slender, no one could wear trains, bustles, and tiptilted little hats with greater effect than could Katharine Cornell.

The play, staged by McClintic, was to have its out-of-town tryout in Albany. The morning of the opening, Kit rose and went moving quickly about the room, her nerves already taut. Presently McClintic heard a bang—and then a low moan.

"What is it?" he asked worriedly.

Kit's dark eyes were bright with pain. "I—I don't know. I just—knocked against the chair. Something's happened. I can't—I—can't—breathe. My side—oh, God, it hurts!"

She sank weakly upon the couch, her face ashen. McClintic lost no time in calling the hotel doctor. After a quick survey the physician announced that she had a broken rib.

"A broken rib!" she gasped. "Why, all I did was knock against a chair!"

"You have a broken rib," he repeated stubbornly.

"But I've got to give a show tonight! And—and how can I when—when I can scarcely move? Every time I turn, every time I breathe—"

"Postpone the opening," he advised.

"No, no, that's impossible."

"Well, we can just take you to the hospital, young woman, and tape you up. I think perhaps you'll be able to play all right."

When Franchot Tone and Rollo Peters, members of the

cast, heard that Kit was in the hospital, they gazed at each other starkly and one of them muttered, "Good Lord!"

Reading their thoughts, Gertrude spoke crisply. "Don't you worry. Miss Cornell will give a show—rib or no rib!"

Sure enough, shortly before the stage manager called "Half hour," there was Kit, her body bandaged, but she was smiling, and assuring everyone that she was quite all right and no one was to worry about her. She felt fine, she insisted, and went to her dressing room where Eveline had hung up the luscious new gowns and laid out her make-up.

Removing her street dress was torture, and when it was off and she stood there in her slip, weakness forced her to lean against—anything. Unfortunately, she leaned against a hot pipe. Instantly, she moved away from it, groaning.

"What is it?" queried Gertrude.

"My arm—that pipe—"

"Good Lord, Kit! Look how you've burned your arm!"

"Miss Cornell!" Eveline scolded, as if Kit were a small, naughty child, "I should think you'd be *careful!*"

She pushed forward a chair and Kit sank into it, her face livid, her eyes spangle-bright with suffering.

"We'll have to fix it up somehow," she told them. "There's no time to talk about it."

"Half hour!" called the stage manager, as if in verification of her words.

It was indeed an ugly burn, but Eveline ran to the drugstore, fulfilling Gertrude's orders, and they managed to ease the pain somewhat with ointments. Minutes were precious now. A new play was opening, and its success or failure depended largely upon the star.

One could scarcely expect a star with a burned arm and

a broken rib to give a brilliant performance, but the curtain
went up on time, and the audience saw a vividly beautiful
Ellen Olenska, moving, laughing, weeping, loving—the very
incarnation of grace.

On November 27, 1928, the play opened in New York
at the old Empire Theater. Entering the star dressing
room, Katharine Cornell stood for a moment in silent
tribute to the many great players who had occupied it in
the past: John Drew, Maude Adams, Billie Burke, Hol-
brook Blinn, Ethel Barrymore, Olga Nethersole, Lionel
Barrymore, Julia Marlowe, Ellen Terry, William Faversham, Mary Boland, Edna Wallace Hopper, William
Gillette, Blanche Bates, Otis Skinner, Bernhardt, Nazimova, Elsie Ferguson, Jane Cowl, Mrs. Fiske, Henry
Miller, Viola Allan. They had all dressed in this room.

Here, they, too, had undergone that fearful trepidation
and suspense of a first night. Here they had known triumph. The theater had been built for the great Charles
Frohman back in 1893, the year of Booth's death. Many
were the great plays which had been produced in the fine
old playhouse since then, and "The Age of Innocence"
came now to take its place among them. For twenty-six
weeks New York, in that age of sophistication, loved "The
Age of Innocence." Flappers with their flimsy, knee-length
skirts crowded the Empire to see Katharine Cornell in
trains and bustles and velvets.

After touring some weeks in "The Age of Innocence,"
Kit followed it with "Dishonored Lady," a modern play
which was sheer melodrama. By 1930 it was the opinion of
Broadway that people would go to see Katharine Cornell
regardless of the vehicle she chose.

People were asking just what it was that made Katharine Cornell sure-fire "box office." What was it about her that drew crowded houses night after night even in a play considered inferior? Everyone had a different explanation. There were those who proclaimed that it was simply magnetism; others decided that it was something called "emotional intensity"; still others maintained that it was both these plus the fact that Katharine Cornell was an "intelligent" actress. There were those, too, who asserted that this popularity could not last, that the public would tire of her and that in a year or two more she would lose her drawing power. They were to be proven wrong, for rather than diminishing, that drawing power increased with the years, emerging triumphant even above financial depressions and war scares, for as a figure in the theater, Katharine Cornell had an ageless, timeless quality.

Now, in 1930, she was definitely established and she was receiving all the attention which her position demanded. Mail poured in to her—fan letters, begging letters, invitations to parties and dinners.

Playwrights, known and unknown, deluged her with manuscripts, for by now it had become almost proverbial that a play in which Katharine Cornell appeared could not fail. Long since, motion picture producers had been offering her fabulous sums for a single picture. Money not being the prime motive of her life, she steadfastly rejected them all.

There were those who declared that she considered herself too highbrow to appear in movies. This was untrue. Next to detective stories, she loved the movies, and went to see them at every opportunity, but she simply had no desire to act in them. The stage had been her first love, and she reacted strongly to the *"feel"* of an audience.

When the movies became talkies she was more in demand than ever, for her voice—vibrant, rich and flexible—was one of her chief attractions. Knowing the part it played in her career, she had taken excellent care of her voice. It was about this time that she discovered that it helped to read French aloud before a performance. One of Katharine Cornell's chief charms as an actress is the apparently unstudied flawlessness of her diction, but the voice itself, beautifully placed and skillfully controlled, was like a well-trained servant, an instrument by which she achieved often masterly effects.

Whether the house be packed or not, a careless, slipshod performance was impossible for her. It did not matter, either, how long she played a single part; like Henry Irving, she played it better at the end of a run than at the beginning. The part itself was continuously ripening and unfolding within her, never did it grow stale. People wondered at that, for the majority of actors playing a part for any length of time grow tired of it, grow careless, and the part becomes after a while like a sucked orange which they are eager to toss aside.

After its New York run, "Dishonored Lady" went on tour to the coast. Kit and Gert made the trip to California by boat that year, and sitting in her deck chair Kit idly fingered a manuscript which had been given her just before leaving. Naturally, she was on the quest for a new play, and had read many only to return them as unsuitable.

The manuscript on her lap now had already been to twenty-seven managers, and twenty-seven times it had been rejected as no good, and, what was even more important, of no box office value.

She lifted her eyes to gaze languidly over the tranquil sea through which even now the setting sun was cutting a path of shimmering gold all the way to the horizon. Oh, but it was good to relax for a time, good to hear no other sound but the drowsy swish of the water against the sides of the boat, good to chat of inconsequential things with Gertrude, good to be free of demands upon her. Guthrie was in California, and she thought of him tenderly, wondering what he was doing and looking forward to joining him.

Again, lazily, contentedly, she glanced down at the manuscript in her lap. On its blue paper cover were the typewritten words:

THE BARRETTS OF WIMPOLE STREET
by
RUDOLPH BESIER

CHAPTER THIRTEEN

"THE BARRETTS OF
WIMPOLE STREET"

I'VE FOUND a play for you!" Kit exclaimed happily, when McClintic met her as she stepped off the boat in California. "A beautiful play, isn't it, Gert?"

"Grand. We read it again and again. Kit's bought it!"

"Bought it?"

"Yes," answered Kit. "The minute I read it I started cabling. It's ours."

"Something for you?"

"Oh, heavens, no! Not for me. I bought it for you. There's nothing in it for me. Oh, Guthrie, I can't wait till you read it!"

But that first day in California was so full that it was not until after breakfast next morning that McClintic began to read. Like two bright, well-behaved children Kit and Gert sat facing him.

"Read it out loud," begged Kit.

He read, and having finished the first act, closed the manuscript holding his place with his thumb, and looked across at his wife.

"Well?" she asked, and her voice had a breathless quality

"You'll do Elizabeth," he answered quietly, as if everything were already settled.

"Oh, no, Guthrie! It's not my kind of part. I could never do Elizabeth Barrett!"

"Why not?"

"Well, because—because I just can't see myself playing it."

But on finishing the play McClintic had his own opinion about that. He was determined that Kit should play Elizabeth Barrett, and she finally yielded to his judgment as she generally did.

Although "Dishonored Lady" was booked until December 20th when it was to close in Boston, they began to plan the production of "The Barretts" at once. It made no difference to either Kit or Guthrie that this play which they considered beautiful had been rejected by twenty-seven supposedly astute managers. They had a firm faith in their own judgment; and now the more Kit studied the part of Elizabeth the more eager she was to play it. It was not enough merely to study the part; she read all she could find about Elizabeth Barrett, for these days her entire world pivoted about that lovely, frail, Victorian figure.

One day, while musing upon Elizabeth, another thought came to her. She looked up at her husband, her eyes as alight as those of a child.

"Guthrie!" she exclaimed, "Guthrie, *this is it!*"

He smiled, that slow smile of his that surged up in his eyes before it got down to his lips. "I was thinking the very same thing, Kit! This is what you've been waiting for. This is the time."

"And this is the play!"

They were silent for long, pulsing moments. The decision had been made. Now all that remained to do was get in touch with Stanton Griffis and Conger Goodyear and announce the fact that the McClintics were ready. From now on instead of

"KATHARINE CORNELL IN . . .

programs would read:

"KATHARINE CORNELL PRESENTS . . ."

The very thought of it was stimulating. This was their great adventure. There was the possibility that it would fail and that they would lose every dollar, but they steadfastly refused even to consider such a contingency. Katharine Cornell had never approved of the star system. To say "Katharine Cornell presents . . . ," thus establishing herself as an actress-manager, was the fulfillment of a long ambition. This sort of billing did not necessitate her having the leading role. An actress, provided she is financially equipped to do so, can present plays all her life, but there might easily come a time when she might have to step down from stardom, when she might be only too glad to support some younger star in a mother role or, for instance, to play the nurse to some new, as yet unknown, Juliet. The loss of beauty or youth need never interfere with the standards or the success of a topnotch producer. And if that producer happens to be an actress, she can assign to herself whatever roles her judgment and heart dictate, and feel proud of her integrity in so doing. So reasoned Katharine Cornell.

Naturally, there were well-meaning friends who strongly advised against the undertaking.

"This is the worst time you could possibly choose. For heaven's sake, if you must manage your own plays, why pick a time like this? After all, this is 1930. Haven't you heard there's a financial depression? Haven't you seen people selling apples on every street corner? Who knows what Hoover will do? All this upheaval! There's no use shutting your eyes to the fact that the country's practically on the eve of a revolution. Why choose *now* to risk all that you've worked so hard for?"

"In these modern days," put in another, "who cares about Elizabeth Barrett? She's passé. Nobody even reads her stuff any more. Only the Browning Societies will be interested, and they're too few to support a play."

But Katharine Cornell, Guthrie McClintic, Conger Goodyear, Stanton Griffis, and Gertrude Macy went calmly on with their plans—for at Gert's request, the others had agreed to let her buy a small percentage of the production. They had come to *believe* in success. Their watchword was progress, not stagnation. Wise, skeptical Broadway read of the project and shrugged. "They'll lose their shirts," announced Broadway.

The five partners only smiled. They were in complete accord. Now was the time when they were to give positive proof that they were not motivated by the money question. True to her decision, Kit declared that the salary which she was at present receiving from Gilbert Miller in "Dishonored Lady" would continue to be all that she would take. In turn, Goodyear, Griffis and Gert gave proof of their disinterestedness by agreeing that if there should be profits, they would receive only the amount of their investment, after that every cent was to be put back into the business. There was but one object—to produce worthwhile plays.

When all business details had been settled and the "Dishonored Lady" came to the end of her storm-tossed days, it was necessary to begin at once upon the all-important problem of casting. Where would they find the ideal man to play the charming Robert Browning? On this quest, McClintic sailed for England. Well-known actors both in America and abroad were eager to play the part, but McClintic was not to be swayed by names.

He wanted the ideal Robert Browning and it did not matter whether the actor who impersonated Browning were famous or not. He found his Browning, finally, in Brian Aherne.

Again the wiseacres of Broadway scoffed. "Whoever heard of this Brian Aherne, anyway?" they asked. "What's he ever done? Why trust a big part like that to someone unknown?"

The producers were unmoved by all this. Another casting problem faced them now, and that was Flush. Flush was the name of Elizabeth Barrett's dog, a cocker spaniel. They advertised for Flush and they found him at last in a five-month-old pup with a love for all the world.

The time for rehearsals had come. Members of Katharine Cornell's companies say of her that she is "easy to work with," which is the theater's way of saying that she is quite devoid of the usual star airs. Her attitude during rehearsals is friendly, quiet, considerate.

Now that she was her own manager, rehearsals took on an amiable pattern. As much as possible, her own scenes were rehearsed at home alone with McClintic, a procedure which shortened the time of rehearsing for the members of her company.

The custom was inaugurated at this time that during the first week of rehearsals the actors did no acting. For the first six days they congregated in the dining room of the Beekman Place house reading the play and discussing it. By 1930 the McClintics had the house to themselves, and a new and satisfactory plan had gone into effect. The two lower floors, used for living and dining, were shared. Kit took the third floor for herself, the fourth floor was done over for McClintic, and Gert rented the fifth floor.

It was an ideal arrangement. Guthrie and Kit could be together when they liked. They took all their meals together, but Kit, returning home tired from a performance, liked to go to bed, while McClintic loved to read in bed and to turn on the radio at all hours. This now he was free to do, and Kit often declared that the house and this arrangement had done much toward making their marriage a success.

The library, the most lived-in room of all, was large, high-ceilinged, graciously proportioned. Its fireplace, framed by an old-fashioned marble mantelpiece, was flanked by well-filled bookcases. At the rear of the room, French windows opened upon a terrace which overlooked the sweep of the busy East River, with cargo boats from all over the world passing and repassing. The furniture was large, built for comfort—deep, roomy chairs, wide couches, tall vases filled with flowers. It was a room which sang out a friendly "hello" to the stranger, cheerily inviting him to come in and rest awhile.

Here or in the dining room the actors met for the first six days, reading their parts and discussing the play. During this interval their parts became familiar to them, and in consequence when they came to rehearse on the stage, their familiarity with the lines permitted them to give undivided attention to the acting itself. The procedure worked so well that it was adhered to for all the plays which were to follow.

Cornell-McClintic rehearsals do not take place in the old-fashioned way on a bare stage with stage braces designating the entrances and exits. An actual set with proper entrances is provided. Provided, too, are any swords, books, and so forth, anything which would come under the heading of a prop. Though Kit rehearses in street clothes, should the part she plays require a hoop skirt, a train, or some article of clothing to which she is unaccustomed, she has its equivalent constructed for rehearsals, attaching it over her street clothes.

This manner of rehearsing accustoms the actors to the use of all things which they will wear or handle during the actual performance. Nothing is strange to them at the opening performance.

With the ending of each day's rehearsal, Kit returned to Beekman Place and to study. Closeted in her own apartment, she would walk back and forth, declaiming. She studied in bed. She liked to be cued in her lines by Gert. Hours upon hours before the fireplace she and Guthrie discussed costumes, sets, colors, the cast. Believing that her husband's taste was above reproach, Kit usually deferred to his judgment, especially in the matter of colors.

"A successful marriage," she declared, "means as much to a woman as being successful in her profession."

"But what is the recipe for a successful marriage?" asked a friend one day.

"Trust," she answered, "trust in each other—and—understanding. Both Guthrie and I love the theater intensely, and we'll sacrifice anything for it. Sacrifice? It isn't *really* sacrifice. We don't regard it as a sacrifice at all. Guthrie gives me confidence and gives me courage. He believes in me. I'd rather work with him than with anybody in the world. He has helped me more than I can say. I depend upon him—upon his direction, his criticisms. Our work comes first, you see, with both of us. It has drawn us closer and closer together. We each regard our job as our life. We've never wanted any other life, we've never wanted any other job."

There was a day during rehearsals of "The Barretts" when things were going badly, when Kit felt unable to express all that she knew the character demanded. Desperately, suffering acutely, she dropped the part and cried out: "I simply cannot play this part! I can't do it! I can't do it as it *should* be!"

Quietly, with a slow and knowing smile, McClintic picked up the part and handed it to her. "You don't mean that you *can't*," he told her calmly, "you just mean that so far you never *have!*"

One of the most important members of the cast was Flush. At first they made a strenuous attempt to hire a professional dog trainer. This was unsuccessful due to the fact that there was, apparently, no dog trainer in New York City who would be free to attend rehearsals for from eight to ten hours a day. Here, indeed, was a quandary. Flush had to know his part and who was to train him? He was only a pup and so far he had never been out of a kennel.

Gertrude Macy loved dogs and understood them. It was she who now stepped forward, volunteering to undertake Flush's education. The first thing she did was to house-break him, which required only three days. Next, she took him to rehearsal every day. It did not take Flush long to become acquainted with the cast, and he soon grew to look forward to the little lumps of raw beef which Gert gave him as a reward for good behavior. Now and then when he was difficult, he received a gentle tap on the nose, which he came in time to recognize as a kindly rebuke.

At first they leashed him in his basket where he was expected to remain during the first scene, but soon he began to understand that he was expected to remain there quietly and the leash was no longer necessary. Dogs are all eager to please, and Flush was no exception. There was one scene where he was supposed to walk off the stage following Wilson, the maid. When he did this correctly, there never failed to be a small piece of meat waiting for him in the wings, and Gert's voice saying softly, "Good dog. Good Flush." Gert found him easy to train, and the entire company was amazed at how easily and quickly he learned his part.

Then there was the absorbing question of costumes.

Correct costuming of a play is as important as the play itself. Before Equity contracts went into effect, actresses were compelled to furnish their own costumes if the play were modern. This was decidedly unfair, for if the play was what was termed a "society drama," the costumes had to be costly. The actress was forced to go into debt to procure suitable costumes for a play which might, and often did, close after a week or two. Fortunately, Equity had remedied this. Nowadays a producer must pay for all wearing apparel that is visible. This includes shoes and stockings and even underwear if it is seen. If an actress is playing an important role, she is privileged to select her own clothes, but less important actresses have their clothes selected and designed by the costume designer whom the management has engaged. In choosing the colors for the actresses' wardrobe the designer must take into consideration the colors of the settings. Too, she must be mindful of the colors chosen by the star and the leading players. Wigs, purses, hats are also supplied by the management, whether the play is a costume play or not.

At last, at long last, the big night arrived.

Everyone was satisfied with the result of the out-of-town opening in Cleveland. Then came New York, and the famous old Empire Theater.

Walking to the theater through the rain that night the actors were hopeful. They are superstitious folk. A pair of shoes on the make-up shelf, a broken mirror, a peacock feather, are ill omens. Whistling in the dressing room is a sure sign that the one nearest the door will shortly receive his two weeks' notice. But rain on an opening night is auspicious; consequently, the harder it poured, the more the actors blessed the rain.

When Kit was a very little girl she used to say the old

singsong refrain which little girls have chanted since time
immemorial:

> Rain, rain, go away,
> Come again some other day.

But now, excitedly, she laughed back at the rain as her
car deposited her before the stage entrance on that early
February night in 1931. She was nervous, tense. Never had
there been so much at stake as there was tonight. Goodyear's money, Griffis' money, Guthrie's money, Gert's
money, her own money. Involuntarily she turned to a
Power beyond herself. "Oh, God," she muttered desperately, "please let everything go—all right!"

Elizabeth Barrett was one of the most difficult parts she
had played. Not only was it an extraordinarily long part,
but Elizabeth was almost constantly on the stage. An actress can depict a character by showing the way the character walks as well as the way she talks. This was impossible
in the case of Elizabeth, for Elizabeth Barrett was an invalid
remaining in a semi-reclining position on a couch during
the first two long scenes of the play.

When the performance had ended, enthusiastic friends
crowded into Kit's dressing room. They kissed her, shook
hands with her, embraced her. She laughed, thanked them
for their tributes, said gay, bright things, realizing all at once
how tired she was, inexpressibly tired. She did not know
yet, no one knew, whether the play was to succeed or not.
Tomorrow's papers would tell that—and it seemed an
eternity until tomorrow.

Drinking, carousing at night clubs, had never the slightest appeal for Katharine Cornell, and now, when at last her
friends were gone, and Eveline had helped her remove

Elizabeth's many petticoats and flounces, Kit, Gert, Guthrie, Griffis and Goodyear drove quietly back to Beekman Place. Since the McClintics had taken the house, the neighborhood had undergone a complete transformation. The slums had been cleared away. Some of the old houses had been restored, others had been torn down and replaced with towering apartment houses. Beekman Place had become one of the smartest residential districts in New York. At this hour of the night everything was very quiet. Occasionally came the sound of the boat horns on the river, but even the rain had ceased, and except for the boat horns and the crackling of the fire, the world seemed very, very still.

The five friends grouped themselves comfortably and informally about the fireplace, talking the whole thing over—every scene, almost every line of the play. As they sat there, Aherne, also unable to think of sleeping, joined them.

"Stanton says he thinks the play won't succeed," Kit announced. "What do you think, Brian?"

"Heaven knows. It's in the lap of the gods. What do you think, yourself, Kit?"

"I don't dare think. I don't know. One can't tell."

As she spoke the bell rang, and a moment later Alexander Woollcott walked in.

"It was wonderful," he declared before anyone even had a chance to greet him. "It was wonderful. You were gorgeous, Kit. The audience loved it. I loved it. We all loved it. Everybody will love it!"

He was speaking the words of truth.

The newspapers were as enthusiastic as Woollcott himself. Brooks Atkinson wrote in the *New York Times*: ". . . Miss Cornell might be showier, but she could hardly be more discriminating, true and exacting. The Barretts of Wimpole Street is a triumph for her and the splendid company with which she has surrounded herself . . . Her acting is quite as remarkable for the carefulness of its design as for the fire of her presence."

In spite of the depression "The Barretts of Wimpole Street" ran at the Empire for over a year. A film producer offered Katharine Cornell three hundred thousand dollars to appear in the movie of the play. Hundreds of people were turned away at every performance. Standing room was sold until every space was filled. Theatrically, it was a bad year. Many Broadway playhouses closed, yet "The Barretts" went on, and could have continued even longer, but Katharine Cornell wanted other cities to see the play she loved.

"The theater does not belong to Broadway," she maintained, "but to all America."

So, with the help of Ray Henderson, she planned a two-year tour. Now that she was a manager in her own right, it was necessary for her to have a press agent. She wanted the best she could find, and she found him in Ray Henderson. Henderson was a tall, scholarly-looking man with sandy-colored hair, a small, neat mustache, and large blue eyes. He dressed conservatively, and never wore any but a bow tie. When something aroused his interest, his enthusiasm was explosive and infectious.

He was honestly enthusiastic about Katharine Cornell. He had seen her in everything she had done. As press representative for William Faversham back in 1916 he had seen her with the Washington Square Players. E. H. Sothern and Julia Marlowe, Forbes-Robertson, Maxine Elliot, Winthrop Ames, Faversham, all of these had profited by the wisdom of Henderson, all these had relied upon him, all these he had served, but none had he served more faithfully, more zestfully, than he now served Katharine Cornell. To him, she was not only a great actress, she was a wonderful being. He wanted not only all America to see her, but even now it was his dream that someday all the world would see her. Why not a world tour? True, no American actress had ever considered such a thing before, but why shouldn't it be done?

As summer approached and it was decided to continue the run of "The Barretts" through the hot weather, Henderson was frankly worried about Kit. She was not looking well. Her usual verve and freshness were lacking. Nights after the play she and McClintic drove to the house they had taken at Sneden's Landing, twenty miles from New New York. Kit, always wanting to be near the water, loved the simple country house which faced the broad, ever-tranquil Hudson. It was an old house—old, small, unimpressive. Here, all day long she would lie listlessly reading. At night they would return to the theater where, in the insufferable heat of New York's midsummer, she would spend three hours being Elizabeth, her body half covered with a woolen afghan.

She began to complain of a pressure at the back of her neck, a constant vibration in her head. It never let up. It was with her as she drove into the country, as she spoke her lines on the stage. She had almost never been ill, and she kept telling herself that it would go away. But it did not. It grew worse.

Gertrude, McClintic, Henderson, Eveline, they were all looking at her anxiously. She was getting alarmingly thin. That strange drumming in her head gave her no rest. The strain began to tell in her face. She who had seemed ageless, now seemed older than her thirty-three years. They begged her to go to a doctor. She saw two. They gave her little satisfaction, and insisted that she must *rest*. Her husband, Gert, Henderson kept telling her to close the show, but she could not endure the thought of throwing her fellow-actors out of work. Times were bad. The welfare of the entire organization depended upon her. She tried massage, which gave only scant relief.

Finally the theater suddenly closed. For the first time in her career, Katharine Cornell had to close because of illness. She had at last yielded to the pleas of her husband, of Gert and Henderson, on one condition: that the actors were to continue to receive their salaries. The other three realized the fairness of this and readily agreed. They planned for her five weeks of complete relaxation. Bermuda, quaint and peaceful, would be an ideal place to rest, they thought.

In Bermuda there were no responsibilities, no cares, no problems. Here there was nothing to do but be very still and very comfortable in socks, low heels, sweaters. But instead of getting better, the awful thumping in Kit's head grew worse. Gert was worried, more worried than she had ever been in her life. Kit did not want to talk about it, but she was suffering intensely and she was frightened.

At last Gert sent for the Swedish masseuse who had helped Kit in New York. The woman took the plane for Bermuda at once. "Ah, this heat!" she exclaimed almost the minute after she had landed, "she'll never get well in this heat. It's too enervating. What she needs is a more stimulating climate like Lake Placid!"

Though they had rented a house and had only spent two weeks in it, Gert had their things packed and a few days later they were on a plane bound for Lake Placid. Seemingly, the masseuse had been right, for once in Lake Placid the fearful thumping in Kit's head began to subside. There were whole days when she scarcely felt it at all, and after three weeks she came back to New York rested, refreshed, vigorous, feeling her old self again.

"The Barretts" reopened and finished out its run. People tried to tell her that it was foolish to take the play away from New York when it was playing to capacity houses, when it was still drawing twenty thousand dollars a week into the box office, and could easily remain for another entire year on Broadway, but Kit was determined to carry out her plan for a tour.

The night of "The Barretts'" closing in New York was a truly festive occasion. The theater was crowded. Kit's dressing room was banked with flowers. Backstage was filled with actors, even those who were working at other houses took time to rush to the Empire only to watch a scene or two.

When the play was over, curtain calls seemed endless. Even Flush, who by now had become a father, was permitted a curtain call with one of his puppies. Friends and admirers swarmed backstage. There was a buzz of talk and laughter. An hour passed.

Outside it was raining. A crowd standing at the stage entrance shivered under their umbrellas, for the night was cold. A bit worried, the stage doorman told Kit about it.

"They've been waiting there for a long time, Miss Cornell. They won't go until they see you. They're yelling their heads off for you."

"Yes, yes, I'll come—right now."

As she followed him toward the stage door, she could hear the cries of the crowd: "Cornell! Bravo, Cornell!"

Then the stage door opened and silhouetted against the lights stood an entrancing figure in the costume of Elizabeth Barrett. She was so lovely standing there, her head up, smiling at them all. The cries of appreciation rose in a glad crescendo.

"Cornell! Cornell! Bravo, Cornell!"

"There isn't much I can say to you now," she told them simply, "except—good-by. But I'll be back after the tour is over. You've all been so wonderfully kind to me!"

Then the stage door closed, the crowd dispersed.

Next day the tour began. She loved the road as much now as she had in "The Man Who Came Back" days. To Kit, sleeping on trains, arriving in strange towns, making up in strange dressing rooms, packing, unpacking— all this would never grow stale. She loved, too, the *feel* of new audiences.

The audience-reaction to the actor is a tepid thing compared to the actor-reaction to an audience. Nothing so stimulates and inspires an actor as an appreciative audience. Leaving the stage after a scene and passing a co-worker in the wings, an actor will exclaim, "Gee, they're *wonderful* to work to tonight!" and his eyes will glow, his step will be buoyant—he will *feel* like acting. Yet another audience will chill him, and he will inform his fellow-trouper that, "They're *handcuffed* out there!" But warm or cold, the modern audience is unfailingly well behaved in comparison to the audiences of even sixty years ago. In the old days if an audience did not approve of the actor, it showed its dislike by hurling at him soft tomatoes, putrid cabbages and rotten eggs. Strangely enough the actor of yesteryear did not dread this barrage of edibles so much as he did the hiss. Superb though his poise might be, it rarely survived the crushing insult of the hiss.

Polite as are modern audiences, however, they have still something to learn in the matter of courtesy. A true actor does not blame a restless audience, for he realizes that this restlessness is a reflection upon him. It indicates that he is losing his hold over his audience, that the fault lies in *him*, and he exerts himself still harder. Yet there are certain discourtesies often indulged in by a small portion of an audience which not only annoy the audience as a whole, but are disconcerting to the actor; such as arriving late after the curtain has risen, whispering, coughing, opening candy boxes and rustling paper during a quiet scene.

Much has been said and written about the debt which an actor owes his audience, but the audience also owes a debt to the actor—for though an audience can always walk out on an actor, the actor can never walk out on an audience.

On this tour Katharine Cornell played to many audiences, good and bad. And it was inevitable that the "audience-pest" should bob up like the proverbial bad penny. The "audience-pest" is the paper-rustler; the cougher; the party which arrives late and then holds lengthy conversations as to who shall sit next to whom; the person who tells his friend in loud whispers the story of the play and what he has seen the actor in before.

Katharine Cornell accepts the audience-pest with more equanimity than do many others of the profession.

"Always remember," she would tell the young novices who asked her advice, "that while you give much to your audience, your audience gives much to you."

When the show played Buffalo, a stout, white-haired man stood in the wings. Listening to the applause which followed each act, "Doc" Cornell remembered a rather pathetic, long-legged child who always felt unpopular with associates of her own age, a child of intensity and restlessness. That child had now become one of America's greatest actresses.

"She has come into her own," he acknowledged gravely.

But after two months the headaches returned, worse now than ever. Fear clutched at her. What was this? Was she losing her mind? Was it a tumor on the brain? She dreaded seeing another doctor. What would he tell her?

Finally in Baltimore she consulted two doctors. One was a general diagnostician, who called in an orthopedic specialist. The latter found that the pain at the back of her head (there was even a lump which was not hard to locate), was a form of occupational neurosis like housemaid's knee or writer's cramp or weaver's bottom. Toscanini once had it in his right arm from wielding the baton. It was thought that Kit's suffering came as the result of projecting her voice and personality to the back rows of the theater for almost two hours, eight times a week, from her particular reclining position on the sofa. The suggested cure was to reverse the set and the sofa so that she could equalize the strain of the muscles on the other side of her neck and head. But there was another kind of strain which the physicians took into account, and that was the strain of feeling that she must keep her actors working no matter what happened. It was the strain of an intense feeling of responsibility.

How, she wondered, could she avoid that feeling of responsibility for which she was paying so high a price? Gert, McClintic, Henderson, Kit, all conferred.

"Suppose," one of them suggested, "we were to engage the company only from one two-week period to the next? If the company understands that, we'd be free to close at the end of each two weeks in case Kit's health does not improve."

They all agreed that the suggestion was worth trying. The company proceeded on this basis for a time; gradually Kit began to feel better and put on weight—she gained eight pounds in two weeks. Soon the headaches were over and she was entirely free, free to enjoy acting and traveling, free to play golf whenever an opportunity to do so presented itself.

She even managed to take ten golf lessons from Ernest Jones. He was enthusiastic about Kit's game. If she would give up the stage, he declared, she could be a champion golfer. He called her attention to the way he lifted his club, bringing it so low that it struck against his back.

"You have a natural swing," he told her, "but don't make

the mistake of trying to imitate. I've noticed that beginners always try to imitate those at the top. Beginning golfers all try to use their clubs as champions do, but it only holds them back. It's always the *eccentricities* which the beginner notices and tries foolishly to copy."

Driving away from the course, Kit spoke thoughtfully. "He's right, Gert. That's true of acting just as it is of golf. The expert is good *in spite* of his flaws. But the novice, watching him, sees those flaws and copies *them*."

In all her long association with Katharine Cornell, one of the things which Gert would never forget was that which happened one afternoon when they were driving to the matinee. Neither she nor Kit had anything to worry about that day. They were both in excellent health, the weather was perfect, the house was already sold out.

As the car moved through the street, Kit glanced at the door. "That door isn't quite closed," she murmured and leaned forward, opening it.

A second later she was lying back, half fainting. No need for Gert to ask what had happened. In fact, in order to release Kit's hand, Gert was compelled to open the heavy door. It was obvious that the bone in the finger was broken, the finger itself was smashed.

"Good Lord, Kit! I've got to get you to a doctor right away!"

Kit still had enough strength to gasp that there wasn't time, that they had to give a show.

"Drive to the nearest drugstore," ordered Gert. "Hurry!"

Kit's face was like a death mask. She sat there, writhing with pain. When the car pulled up before a drugstore, Gert sent the chauffeur for aromatic spirits of ammonia, and went herself to telephone for a doctor. The ammonia revived Kit somewhat and when they reached the stage entrance, she was able to walk to her dressing room. The doctor arrived almost simultaneously.

The finger was now a curious-looking object. Extending from the tip was a huge round blister which resembled a red balloon. How could Kit give a performance with a hand like that? How could she possibly act while in such excruciating pain?

"Looks like the bone's smashed," the doctor announced.

"But what can you do for her?" cried Gert.

"I can't do anything now. She'll have to go right to the hospital and have it x-rayed."

"No," Kit murmured, "no, there isn't time. In twenty-five minutes I've—got—to—play the matinee!"

"Do something, Doctor!" begged Gert. "How can she play with a hand like that?"

"Well, I'll lance it. I'll lance it now, and then after the show—" he became busy with his instruments, "I'll lance that blood blister now and—"

Kit groaned. "Will I—have to lose the finger?"

"I don't know. We'll wait until we see the x-rays."

No, Gertrude Macy could not easily forget that day. She could not forget the courage of Katharine Cornell as she played the matinee with a handkerchief about her hand. She could not forget those hours later at the hospital, and Kit coming back to the theater that night, and playing for weeks afterward with her hand in a plaster cast.

But the tour was not interrupted.

CHAPTER FOURTEEN

TROUPERS

*I*T'S A darn shame," Ray Henderson was saying one afternoon in Chicago. "Something ought to be done about it."

"The school teachers, you mean?" asked Kit.

"Yes, the teachers. The country's in such a bad way that the Chicago school teachers are being paid with scrip—and most of them are practically without actual necessities. Something ought to be done about it."

"But Ray," Kit answered warmly, "something *can* be done about it—we can do it!"

"How?" asked Gert. "What do you mean?"

"Well, look. We're just finishing our Chicago run. We've done four weeks of terrific business. Ray, how many people do you suppose have wanted to buy the dollar seats and been turned away?"

"I don't know—thousands."

"There you are. Simply amazing. Thousands of people in Chicago with a dollar to spend have tried to see 'The Barretts' and couldn't get in. Well then, why can't we take the biggest place in town and give a Sunday afternoon performance charging a dollar a seat?"

Gert's white teeth flashed in a broad grin. Ray's blue

eyes glowed. Now that his interest was fully aroused, his enthusiasm was so great that he could no longer sit quietly in his chair. He rose and walked excitedly about the room.

"Wait, Kit, I'm way ahead of you. We'll give the show on Sunday. I'll have it announced in the newspapers, in the schools, over the radio. We'll take the Civic Opera House and we'll have no seat over one dollar! We'll—"

Practical as always, Gert broke in to ask how much it would cost to rent the Civic Opera House.

"I don't know." He reached for the phone. "But I'll find out."

A few minutes later he hung up the receiver with the announcement that they could rent the Civic Opera House for a charity benefit for one performance at five hundred dollars.

"Anything over that five hundred," declared Kit, "will go to the Teachers' Sick Fund. I'm sure we can get the company and the staff to donate their services. And another thing, as far as the selling of the tickets is concerned, it will be first come, first served. We'll deal with no ticket speculators."

"Right!" agreed Henderson feelingly. "May I announce that you'll sell the first one hundred tickets, Kit?"

"Sure," she answered readily, "I'll do anything—anything I possibly can to help."

"Okay, then. I'll have the announcement read that tickets will go on sale at ten o'clock Sunday morning and that you'll be in the box office."

When Sunday came, Kit and Gert left their hotel shortly before the appointed time, for it was still Katharine Cornell's rule to be always punctual. So scrupulous is she in her adherence to this rule that she usually finds herself too early for appointments. Now, as they drove toward the Civic Opera House, Gert noticed that Kit was nervous.

"Gert," she admitted at last, in a very small voice, "I'm— frightened!"

Gert smiled at her fondly. "What on earth about? 'Fraid you won't give the right change?"

"No, no, I'm serious. It just occurred to me—suppose nobody comes? The Civic Opera House, do you know how many people it *holds?*"

"Sure. Four thousand."

"Four thousand. That's—a great many people, Gert. Suppose only a thousand or so turn up?"

"Well, suppose only five hundred turn up? We've tried to help. We've seen people in desperate need and we've done what we could to alleviate the situation. We can't do any more than that, can we?"

"*No—except to give the best performance we've ever given in our lives!*"

They were silent for some time. As the car approached its destination, Gert looked at her wrist watch.

"What time is it?" asked Kit.

"A little before ten." She glanced up from her watch. "Good Lord," she cried, "will you look at that?"

Kit followed her gaze, staring into the street unbelievingly. The line had already formed. The people were not standing in single file; instead, the line was ten feet wide and it stretched for three blocks. Kit learned later that the queue had begun to form at five o'clock that morning.

"Oh!" gasped Kit, and then in a rather faint voice, "I think I'd better get out and walk."

"For heaven's sake, why?"

"Well, I think I'd better. Perhaps they'd rather see me *walk* up to the theater. I mean—to drive up—it seems rather—"

"Not at all. You're an actress. They expect glamour from actresses. Stay in this car and *give them glamour!*"

"But I don't want glamour. I loathe it. I—it seems better taste to—"

Gert won the argument. Scarcely had the big, luxurious car stopped at the curb before the word ran from end to end of that long, patient line.

"There she is. Katharine Cornell's just come! She's going into the lobby!"

"Well, she's right on time. They *said* she'd open the box office at ten sharp."

"Yeah. I got a cousin that has a friend that has an aunt that met her once. They say she's a good scout."

"Yeah, I heard that, too. They say she ain't a bit high hat."

"Not her. Here she is, givin' up her Sunday t' help th' teachers. Say, listen, I work hard all week an' when Sunday comes, bullieve you me, brother, I'm only too glad t' get away from it an' take my rest. But not *her!* When Sunday comes, that dame goes right on workin', even when she don't *have* to. Yeah, lookit her now!"

Yes, look at her now. There she was in the box office, gazing down at a large pile of dollar bills to which were pinned slips of paper, each paper having a name written on it.

"What's all this?" she asked.

"Oh, that," answered the attendant, "they're from the

directors—the big shots. They don't want to stand in line."

"Is that so? Nice for the directors. But this is a benefit performance, and if the directors want to see this show, they'll have to stand in line like those others out there."

"Okay, Miss Cornell. Oh, say, the fire chief was around."

"Yes? And what did he want?"

"Seats."

"You mean free seats?"

"He says he's going to have them—or else."

"Or else—what?"

"Or else he'll close the show."

"Well, you tell the fire chief we're sorry, but he won't get any free tickets—and he won't close the show! Is that all the business we have to take care of now?"

"Yes, that's all."

"Then open the window and let's start selling. Those people out there must be tired."

Although modern theaters are completely fireproof, a uniformed fireman is present during every performance. There are usually "No Smoking" signs on the stage. Everyone connected with the theater is extremely conscious of fire hazards where the theater is concerned. No performer would ever think of throwing away a cigarette without grinding it out with his foot. So ingrained does this habit become that an actor will subconsciously step on his cigarette even when throwing it away on the street. Actors usually smoke in their dressing rooms between acts, but if the fireman orders anyone to put out his cigarette, the actor knows that he must do so at once and without argument for, in protection of the public safety, the city fire department has the right to close the theater if the fire laws are not obeyed. The fireman is authorized to arrest any actor who breaks a fire law, thus taking him out of the cast and interrupting the performance.

Before the curtain rang up that day, Katharine Cornell went visiting in every dressing room. She told each player about the fire chief. "We must not give him an opportunity to close the show in the middle of the performance," she insisted. "No matter how much, no matter how terribly you want to smoke, *don't!* Don't smoke backstage or in the dressing rooms! Don't—*please*, don't give that man the slightest chance to make any trouble!"

Everyone solemnly gave his word.

Outside the line continued to grow. Even while the first act curtain was rising, attendants were telling people there were no more seats—no, not even standing room. The line was still more than a block long. When the play was over, the audience not only applauded—they cheered.

Though the fire chief was there, watching everyone very closely, he found no excuse for interfering with the performance.

While Kit was on tour in 1932 the sad news reached her of Jessie Bonstelle's death. Dear, indefatigable Jessie Bonstelle! Everyone in the profession had loved and respected her. Kit's mind went back to those early days in stock when, confronted with some part or some scene which seemed beyond her powers, she would say, "I can't do it!" and calmly, decisively, Jessie would answer, "Of course you can."

Speaking of her friend, Kit said sorrowfully, "She gave me encouragement at a critical time of my life. She did more. She provided the rudiments of my calling. My admiration, my gratitude to Jessie Bonstelle can never be expressed in words. The theater has suffered a severe loss."

The tour came to an end in San Francisco. She was to revive "The Barretts" later, and by the time it finally ended, the show had made one million fifty thousand dollars. Even now, after having played it for so long, she was loath to give up the part of Elizabeth Barrett, for with each performance she had loved it more and more.

Plans being already complete for the following season, the McClintics went to Europe on a holiday. There was a place—a sweet, unfrequented spot in the Tyrol—a quaint Bavarian town called Garmisch. They had passed through it quickly years before, and had promised themselves that someday they would go back there and stay awhile. When they now returned to it, Garmisch was quite as peaceful, quite as lovely, as they had imagined it to be, and they told each other delightedly that they would return to the village again and again. Although Flush was still alive, it was during that first day in Garmisch that Kit annexed four dachshund pups. She had always had dogs, and she, Guthrie and Gert were all dog lovers. The stay in Garmisch lasted three months, after which the McClintics returned to New York, and rehearsals for their next play, "Lucrece."

But though "Lucrece" was a superb and artistic production, the public did not like it, and it ran for only four weeks. This was a disappointment as well as a heavy monetary loss, for "Lucrece" had been a costly venture. No use moaning, however, no use trying to force a run. The only thing to do was to get on to something else; and this something else, in the season of 1933, was a modern play called "Alien Corn."

"Alien Corn" opened its New York run in February, 1933. At this time America was undergoing a turbulent and perilous experience. Franklin Delano Roosevelt was to take the oath of office in March. Meanwhile, in every town and city banks were closing. People were panicky. No one knew whether it was wise to leave money in the banks or whether it was safer to draw it all out and keep it at home. This state of confusion brought runs on many of the remaining banks, which they for the most part were unable to meet.

The crisis came on Saturday, March 4, 1933, when the new President suddenly announced that for a time all banks throughout the entire country would close. Coming without warning, this decree left the majority of people temporarily with no funds.

On the morning of the Bank Holiday, McClintic had sailed for Europe. Ray was out of town; Conger Goodyear, Stanton Griffis and Gert were in Florida. The running of the theater now rested upon Kit, and the announcement of the sudden closing of the banks presented her with a problem such as she had never faced before.

Anxiously, she called Gert over long distance. With the years, Gert's position had undergone several changes. She was stage manager for "The Barretts," a post rarely filled by a woman; since 1932, however, her place had been in the box office rather than backstage, for she had become Katharine Cornell's manager. It was she who made up the payrolls, paid all bills, counted receipts, handled all finances.

"Have we enough cash on hand to pay the salaries tonight?" Kit asked.

Gert's voice was calm. "Yes. Fortunately, I think I must have had a hunch something like this would happen, because I told the box office not to bank the last week's receipts. We didn't draw any money out of the bank last week, but neither did we deposit what we took in. Don't worry, Kit, we've plenty on hand to meet salaries."

"Good. Good."

"Probably tonight there'll be no sale at all. People haven't any money to pay for seats."

"That's all right. I'll tell the box office to trust everybody."

"Trust? For seats? Trust total strangers?"

"Anybody. If ever people needed the theater, needed something to take their minds off their troubles, they need it now. The box office must take anything they give us—checks, I. O. U.s—anything."

"All right, Kit," answered Gertrude crisply, and as she turned away from the phone she had a moment of swift pride in Katharine Cornell. She left Florida that night in order to get back to New York as soon as possible.

Meanwhile, Kit's phone began ringing frantically. Friends who were businessmen sought to advise her, their voices strident with anxiety.

"Better close the show! Give the company its two weeks' notice—*now!* No one knows what's going to happen!"

But Kit stood calm and firm.

"Kit, you're crazy," they shouted. "This attitude of yours is utterly quixotic and impractical. It just proves you don't know a darn thing about business. All right. Say you take in thousands of dollars. What will it be? Money? Of course not. It'll be paper! Paper—from absolute strangers. How do you know you'll ever collect on it?"

But Katharine Cornell stood her ground valiantly. The

show went on. People gave checks and I. O. U.s for seats.
Yet not one dollar did Katharine Cornell lose through
trusting in the honesty of her fellow-man, for when the
banks opened again, every penny was paid.

Twelve weeks ended the run of "Alien Corn" on Broadway, and a short tour followed, for though it was far from
a failure, the play did not approach the spectacular success
of "The Barretts." With the coming of summer, Kit and
Guthrie returned to Garmisch.

For a long time now people had been telling her that
she ought to do Shakespeare, but she had laughed. "No,
no, not I. Shakespeare's not for me," she maintained.

But "Lucrece" had been written in blank verse, and it
was during its brief run that the thought had come to her:
"Perhaps I *could* do Shakespeare, after all!"

So, since McClintic was insisting that she play Juliet,
the vacation in Garmisch was devoted to the study of that
character. Too, Henderson had been talking about a complete transcontinental tour, not a tour which included only
the larger cities, but a tour of the entire country. Such a
tour would require two years. For a long time now the old
theatrical custom of sending out road companies had fallen
into disuse. There were people in the small towns who had
grown to manhood and womanhood without ever seeing
a real play, without ever seeing actors and actresses in the
flesh. This idea of Henderson's was therefore both surpris-
ing and daring, but the more he talked about it, the more
enthusiastic he became—and Henderson's enthusiasm was
as infectious as laughter. He was certain that such a venture
would make money. As he planned the tour, it was to cover
seventeen thousand miles. He himself would travel ahead

as advance man, finding suitable theaters, taking care of advertising, and making hotel arrangements for the company, which would include fifty-two people.

They would present a repertoire of three plays—"The Barretts of Wimpole Street," "Candida" and "Romeo and Juliet." Each play was a costume play, each play required its own properties, its own scenery. The wardrobe included one hundred and twelve costumes. Two baggage cars would be needed for the baggage alone. In addition to the actors, there would be a stage crew which included two wardrobe mistresses, a stage carpenter and assistant, a property man and assistant, two electricians, two stage managers, a company manager, Kit's maid, and five wives who accompanied their husbands. In addition to all this, there would be the dogs. Besides Flush, there were Kit's pet dachshund, and Basil Rathbone's police dog, Moritz. There were two Pullman cars, one of which was all sections, while the other comprised a drawing room, three compartments and eight sections. The scenery, props and electrical equipment were very heavy. It required ten large trucks to carry everything from the baggage cars to the theaters.

The great actors of the past had made such tours year after year. They, too, had had a repertoire of their favorite plays. In the very early days, the days of Junius Brutus Booth and Edwin Forrest, traveling with scenery and a company was unheard of. Towns in those days were fewer, and separated by vast distances. The stars had traveled alone, sometimes by steamboat or barge, sometimes by buggy, sometimes by stagecoach, with only a valise containing their own costumes, for at that time each city had its stock company which "supported" the visiting star.

With the increased facilities in transportation, the road came into its own, and for years the country had been honeycombed with entire companies of players bringing their own scenery and their own troupes. But with the coming of the movies, the theatrical picture had changed, and this form of entertainment had been gradually abolished.

The Cornell tour would begin in Kit's home town, Buffalo, and from there it would visit seventy-five towns and cities. It would include many one-night stands.

"The road doesn't pay any more," was the universal opinion of the managers of New York. "The people want movies, not living actors."

It was not the first nor would it be the last time that Katharine Cornell, ignoring precedent, was to prove the know-it-alls of Broadway wrong. Everywhere she went she played to spectacular business. People drove in from farms, drove for as much as a hundred miles, to see a play with "live" actors. As for the actors, they often dressed in musty-smelling dressing rooms which had not been opened for years. They traveled through sandstorms, floods, sun, blizzards.

On Christmas Eve of 1933 they were frankly homesick. Now and then as the train sped through the countryside they could see homes where, through unshaded windows, they caught brief glimpses of festivities, of Christmas trees and families at dinner. The Cornell Company was on its way from Duluth to Seattle. It was raining—a dismal, cold, steady rain. Men and women sat gazing forlornly out of the car windows, and nobody talked much. Would it never stop raining? The speed of the train was slackening. Now and then an actor rose from his seat and walked impatiently up and down the aisle. Someone said that he felt as if he ought to get out and *push* the train.

"This *slowness!*" sighed another. "It gets on your nerves."

"Conductor," asked Basil Rathbone, the leading man, "what seems to be the trouble? Why are we slowing up like this?"

"Washout ahead," answered the conductor, and hurried forward.

"Conductor," queried a young man as yet unknown, named Orson Welles, "do you think we'll make Seattle on time?"

"Can't say. Likely not. Washout ahead."

McClintic, who had recently joined them so as to be with his wife for the holidays, was bearing it with his usual equanimity. In her stateroom, Kit lifted her eyes from the detective story she was reading, and gazed thoughtfully, pensively, out of the window.

"Tired, Kit?" asked Gertrude Macy concernedly.

"Tired? No, not very. I was just thinking—about the company. They all seem so dispirited. I was thinking, Gert, what they need is a dinner!"

"A dinner?"

"They. Us. All of us. A real Christmas feast, a big dinner with the dining car all to ourselves. Why couldn't we?"

Like Napoleon, Gertrude Macy knows not the word "impossible." She left the stateroom and in less than half an hour she was back, grinning.

"It's okay, Kit. The steward says that after all the other people have left the dining car, we may have it to ourselves!"

"Turkey?"

"Well, no. I'm afraid I couldn't manage the turkey, but they've sent ahead for twenty chickens—and we'll have some punch, too."

With the news of the coming feast, everyone grew brighter. It *was* Christmas, after all. Suddenly it began to *feel* like Christmas. They forgot the rain and they forgot their loneliness when later they gathered in the dining car, eating, laughing, distributing gifts. They forgot, too, the washout ahead and the ever-diminishing speed of the train.

Dinner over, someone began to sing:

> "Holy night, silent night,
> All is dark save the light . . ."

For hours they sang Christmas carols, the waiters standing about joining in. It was suddenly Christmas for them, too. What did it matter that there was a flood ahead? Here in this dining car was that for which Christmas forever stands—peace on earth and good will to men.

At last the actors retired to their berths, for they would reach Seattle tomorrow, Christmas day, at eight in the morning. But when they awoke next day the train was still inching warily along, and in response to anxious questions the conductor said that it would be at least four or five o'clock before they reached their destination. Here and there bridge and poker games were started. Five o'clock came and went, and by eight o'clock everyone knew that giving a show that night was impossible. The train would crawl a few miles, stop, start again. The company began to feel a sharp sense of danger. There were no more games. They knew that ahead of them miles and miles of track had been washed away and that laborers were working in the rain to build trestles over which the train might pass. The rain continued, beating remorselessly and interminably upon the protesting earth.

"Will we give a show?" the company asked Gertrude Macy as she walked through the train.

"I don't know. It's past eight now, and we're still a long way from Seattle."

"For heaven's sake," sighed a woman wearily, "where is this Seattle, anyhow? Does the place actually exist or is it a myth?"

Gloom settled over the entire company. In her state-room, Kit sat motionless, depressed. She asked Gert to tele-graph the Seattle theater manager that she would give a performance if it could start any time before midnight and if he considered it wise to do so.

She had looked forward to Seattle. After all, it was Guthrie's home town. The company was bored with this long trip, and worn with the constant sense of danger. As minutes passed, she grew very tired. Her depression deep-ened. Even talking to Gert and Guthrie was an effort. She tried to read, but all at once the detective story had become unbearably dull.

At eleven-fifteen P. M. the train finally pulled into the Seattle station. The manager of the theater was waiting, and so, he declared, was the audience.

"Waiting?" gasped Kit. "At this hour? Waiting ever since eight-thirty?"

"The house is packed to the rafters, Miss Cornell," affirmed the manager. "I don't expect you people'll feel much like giving a show, but they've been waiting all this time—and hoping."

It was incredible. Kit looked at her husband. "It's up to you, Kit," he shrugged. "It would be easy to send them away if you feel—"

"Send them away?" Kit's head was up and her black eyes were sparkling. "Gert! Tell everybody! *We're giving a show!*"

The baggage men began unloading the cars, the baggage trucks stood waiting. The members of the company were rushed in autos to the theater.

In her dressing room, McClintic looked anxiously at his wife. "It's been a ghastly trip, Kit. How do you feel? All right? Want anything?"

She looked up at him and said meekly, "I wish I had a raw egg."

He laughed. "An egg? Is that all you want? Of course. The simplest thing in the world. I'll get you an egg."

It was not so simple as he had supposed. Every store around the theater district was closed. But Kit wanted an egg and he had promised to get it for her.

Finally he thought of a friend with whom he used to go to school, found a telephone book, phoned the number—and there was no answer. He recalled the name of another boy with whom he had played as a lad, and phoned again, but again there was no response. He made other attempts, and at length a drowsy voice answered.

"Hello!" cried McClintic jubilantly. "Ben? . . . This is Guthrie . . . Guthrie McClintic! . . . I used to go to school with you. Remember Lincoln High? . . . Well—er—the fact is, I'm looking for an egg . . . An egg! . . . I've got to have an egg . . . No, my *wife* wants an egg! Will you lend me an egg? Or can you tell me some place around the Metropolitan Theater where I can buy an egg? . . . You see, we just got in and all the stores are closed . . . Thanks, old man, thanks! You say there's a diner three blocks away? And it's open? . . . Why, of course, they'd have an egg!"

Feeling somewhat like a conqueror now, he raced back to Kit's dressing room. "It's all right, dear. I've got your egg. I mean, I've sent for it and it's coming. Well, I see the stuff's arrived. Record time, too. Those fellows must have *worked!*"

"Guthrie, those poor people sitting out there—they must be so bored. It's almost twelve o'clock. Why not pull up the curtain and let the audience watch the boys setting the stage?"

"Kit," declared her husband admiringly, "you're a regular *trouper!*"

Yes, she was a trouper, this Katharine Cornell. In theatrical vernacular, there is no higher compliment that one actor can pay another than the words: *"You're a trouper."* To be a trouper means to take the bad as gracefully as the good, to make the best of everything, to give a show at all costs, and to meet emergencies victoriously.

But Guthrie McClintic, too, was a trouper. Debonair, friendly, informal, he stepped on the stage.

"Ladies and gentlemen, we thought it might interest you to see what goes on behind the scenes . . . The stage-hand is now bringing in Elizabeth Barrett's couch, and the stage manager is telling him where it must be placed . . . This is Elizabeth's table, there is her oil lamp, her book, her afghan . . . The set which is now being put up is her room. Outside that window is Wimpole Street . . . Do you see this curious contrivance? That's what is called 'a baby spot,' that will produce the effect of sunlight which later you will see streaming in through the window . . . Those big trunks the men are putting in the middle of the stage are the wardrobe trunks . . . The lady now unlocking the trunks is none other than our wardrobe mistress, Johanna Kling. Take a bow, Johanna . . . and here—" his voice took on a very real note of affection, "here, ladies and gentlemen, is one of the most important members of the cast. This is— *Flush!*"

Assisted by the stage manager, McClintic continued this extemporaneous entertainment until one o'clock.

". . . and now, it is one o'clock. The curtain will come down. Five minutes from now it will rise again on—'*The Barretts of Wimpole Street*'!"

And in precisely five minutes, it did rise.

Tired though they were, the actors gave inspired performances. The audience, far from being jaded, was alert, appreciative, enthusiastic, when, at four A. M., the curtain came down, no one wanted to leave. They stood in the aisles and cheered. The curtain went up again and again, the house rocking with applause.

"I've never been so happy in my life," declared Kit laughingly. "I've never been so happy and so tired both at the same time."

"It's been wonderful," declared Welles.

"Wonderful," Kit echoed, "and I'm hungry."

"I'm starving," put in Gert.

"There's a diner a few blocks away," announced McClintic, who had the faculty of always being able to say just the right thing at the right time, "let's all go there and have scrambled eggs and coffee!"

There was a shout from the players, and they rushed to their dressing rooms.

Gert thought of Henderson who, as press representative, was naturally traveling in advance of the troupe.

"Too bad Ray had to miss this," said Gert. "He'd have loved it!"

Greasepaint not wholly removed in their impatience, the actors assembled on the stage half an hour later and walked to the diner in a body. For a minute the owner stood, open-mouthed, looking at them in amazement. So many customers at this time in the morning? But these customers were friendly, laughing folk, calling good-naturedly for scrambled eggs and toast and coffee. As the man worked himself to exhaustion to fill the orders, their merry talk eddied pleasantly about him.

"It's been a grand Christmas!"

"Marvelous. You wouldn't believe such a thing could happen."

"We *did it, didn't* we? We rang up the curtain at five minutes after one in the morning? Sounds utterly fantastic."

"Could it be that this is all a *dream?*"

"What time is it now?"

"Five! Six! Who cares?"

"Ummm, that coffee smells good! I wouldn't change places with anyone right now for anything in the world."

The diner owner shook his head. "Actors," he told himself, "are *funny people!*"

CHAPTER FIFTEEN

JULIET

*U*NTOWARD OCCURRENCES which in the amateur would produce dismay, are taken with a laugh by the seasoned trouper. One-night stands, particularly when continued over a long period of time, are difficult at best. The mere traveling itself is apt to grow unspeakably wearisome. Each town comes finally to seem very like another, and in most instances the actor's path restricts itself to three points—the station, the hotel, the theater. Every theater, however, presents a new problem. Some stages are small, some are large. In some places the acoustics are excellent, in others the acoustics are bad. Some towns are noted for the coldness and unresponsiveness of the audience, while other towns are outstanding for the warmth of the playgoers. The actor adapts himself to all this with a certain amount of grace. It is, he will tell you, "all in the game." He is grateful for, and receptive to, the good that he finds in his wanderings, while he tries to make light of the bad. For instance, in Oakland, the Cornell company played in a large theater. While "Romeo and Juliet" was being presented in half of it, a basketball game was in progress in the other half. Playing Shakespeare with a pistol going off in the big scenes would shake the poise and perhaps even result in hysterics for the tyro, but the real actor continues his performance unshaken, and when it is over can even laugh about it. The Cornell Company could laugh, too, in Colorado Springs where the theater contained only two dressing rooms, forcing all the women to dress together, taking their turns at making up before a single mirror.

In Amarillo, Texas, they played during a duststorm, when sand and wind beating against the theater were so loud that the actors could scarcely hear their cues. Ferocious though the storm was, the theater was packed. Bus loads of people had driven three hundred miles to see "live" actors for the first time. The "live" actors, leaving the theater after the show, found it impossible to breast the tumult of wind and sand, even to walk as far as the curb. It looked as if they would be compelled to remain in the theater all night, until the taxicab drivers of Amarillo came to the rescue, backed their cabs up on the sidewalk as close to the stage door as possible, filled them with actors, and drove through the gale to the hotel. Although there was no rain, they were forced to use their windshield wipers to clear the dust from the windshields.

Back in New York, McClintic was busy producing one of his most artistic successes—"Yellow Jack." Katharine Cornell was always as interested in her husband's work as she was in her own, and as the time for its opening drew near she felt again the fearful tension of the first night. Only when the reviews were sent to her in St. Louis and she knew that it was a triumph for him, did she begin to enjoy the trip again. Town followed town—big towns, little towns—and always interviews, press photographers, crowds;

crowds everywhere, especially around the stage entrances, waiting to see her as she left the theater.

There was an afternoon in Beekman Place when McClintic answered the telephone to hear a clipped voice saying: "Richmond calling. Hold on, please."

He was not apprehensive. Kit's tastes were simple. She liked simple food, simple clothes. She had but one extravagance, and that was long distance telephone calls. Presently he heard her voice—unhurried, cheery.

"Hello."

"Hello, Kit. You're all right?"

She laughed. "Of course, I'm fine. I'm calling from Richmond. Gert and I just got in."

"Gert and you? Where's the company?"

"Oh, they're coming later on a *good* train. Gert and I took a bad train so that we'd be sure to get here on time."

"Time for what?"

"Well, that's what I'm calling you about. You see, Gert had wired ahead for a radio, but when we get here we find that there isn't any in the room."

A puzzled frown began settling over McClintic's face. "You're calling to tell me that you've no radio in your room?"

"Yes, that's it."

"But—aren't there any radios in Richmond?"

"Oh, yes, but it seems they have no national hook-up! And at first I was so disappointed because I thought I couldn't hear the concert."

"What?"

"The concert. Toscanini. It's his last of the season."

McClintic's voice took on a slightly dazed quality. Was

this Kit—his sensible, level-headed Kit—calling him from Richmond merely to tell him that she could not hear a concert over the radio? It did not, he reasoned, make sense. But McClintic, the very soul of patience, asked, "Well, but—what do you want me to do?"

"Would you mind, Guthrie? Just turn on the radio."

"You—want me to turn on the radio? Me? Here in New York? But how will that solve your problem?"

"Oh, perfectly. You just turn on the radio and put the mouthpiece of the phone as close to it as possible. Then I can lie right back here on the bed and have a heavenly time all afternoon listening to the concert!"

"Oh, I see. Yes, of course. Well, how are things going?"

"All right. There were some managers of the movie houses here who swore they wouldn't let us give a show. It looked pretty serious at first, but I called up your uncle, Judge McClintic, in Charleston, and told him all about it. So then he phoned some people he knew here in Richmond and they fixed everything up for us. How are you, anyhow? I can hardly wait to see 'Yellow Jack.' Well, it's almost time for the concert—"

"Yes. Just hold on a minute. I'll move the radio over to the phone. Have a good time!"

"Thanks."

It was, thought McClintic as he moved the radio in line with the telephone, never dull, being married to Katharine Cornell.

"What," an interviewer asked her one day, "is the secret of prolonged youth?"

"Never think of age," she answered readily. "I think

women ought not to have birthday parties. And as for artificial restoratives for youth, it's futile to waste time and money on them. It's not those external things that help. The secret is proper work."

"Work?"

"Work—*with the mind.*"

"And what do you find the most interesting thing of all?"

"Living. Living is interesting—sheer living!"

"And what is your secret for beauty?"

"Beauty? I have no secret for beauty. There is beauty in all people. Oh, yes! It is there, under the surface, perhaps, but we can find it—not only in others, but in ourselves. And then, having found it, treasure it and be true to it in thought and in action—that is the secret of beauty."

On June 20th the tour ended, and Kit declared that she would not have missed it for the world. They had played seventy-five towns and they had grossed six hundred and fifty thousand dollars.

Vacation lay ahead—a lovely, lazy time in Majorca. They had rented a tiny white villa overlooking the Mediterranean, and here, fairly living in a bathing suit, Katharine Cornell planned her coming season. It would be "Romeo and Juliet" for New York, a new and better production.

When the stay at Majorca ended there was a trip by motor to Barcelona, Andorra, Carcassonne, two weeks on the Riviera, then to Geneva and after that, Garmisch again. Garmisch had come to seem as much home to her as was Beekman Place or Sneden's Landing, and here at Garmisch, though she had already played Juliet for over a year, she went to work on the part again, studied works of reference, read books on the period, wandered off away from everybody and went over and over every scene by herself.

How many actresses—good and bad, young and old, famous and unknown—had played Juliet since the first woman, Mrs. Saunderson, had played the role in London in 1662! Charlotte Cushman had chosen to play the part of Romeo, but with this exception the greatest actresses of each succeeding era had played Juliet—and each had given her own personal conception of this enchanting character. It was the part in which the great Fanny Kemble had made her theatrical debut, and it was for her the gateway to fame. The exquisitely lovely Ellen Terry had played it. Maude Adams. Adelaide Neilson. Modjeska. Mrs. Patrick Campbell. Eleanor Robson. Julia Marlowe. Jane Cowl—the list of great Juliets is almost endless.

And now Katharine Cornell was to play it in New York to Basil Rathbone's Romeo, Brian Aherne's Mercutio, and Orson Welles' Tybalt. Before returning to New York she wanted to see the place where the real Juliet had lived, so she hired a Ford, drove down through Ravenna and on to Verona where, just outside the city, still standing, was the home of the wealthy Capulets. Here was the very garden where Romeo had come. There was the very balcony— how small it was, and how high!—where Juliet had stood one moonlit night, and leaning her cheek against her hand, had murmured wistfully:

> "Oh, Romeo! Romeo! Wherefore art thou, Romeo?
> Deny thy father, and refuse thy name;
> Or, if thou wilt not, be but sworn my love,
> And I'll no longer be a Capulet."

Upon Katharine Cornell's return to New York rehearsals began, and finally after strenuous weeks of unremitting toil, came that familiar cry: "*Curtain going up!*"

She had expected to be more nervous upon this occasion than upon any preceding opening night of her career, but never had she been so calm. Not until the performance was over did she betray any sign of strain or anxiety. Gert, coming in to her dressing room after the final curtain had been rung down, found her in tears.

"What in the world are you crying for?" asked Gert. "The house was packed. They liked it. Couldn't you *tell* how much they liked it?"

"Yes. Yes. They were kind. I felt that they liked us. I don't know why I'm crying. I just am."

But she stopped almost at once, removed her make-up, and went home to Beekman Place. Friends dropped in, all enthusiastic about the production, but all curious as to the criticisms which would appear in the next day's papers. At last they were gone, and the old house was very still.

After a first performance, many actors sit up all night waiting for the first edition of the morning papers. Though McClintic has been known to do so, Katharine Cornell never does.

"Shall we sit up and wait for the morning papers?" asked McClintic, now.

"What time is it?"

"Three."

"I think I shall go to bed."

And she did.

But at seven-thirty Kit was wide awake. Footsteps were tiptoeing past her door. She smiled, knowing that it was

Guthrie on his way to get the morning papers. She waited
expectantly. Presently she heard him tiptoeing back. For
a moment he listened at her door, and then he opened it,
his voice ringing out jubilantly.

"I don't care whether you're awake or not! You've got to
read them! They're marvelous!"

She sat up in bed. He pulled up a chair and began to
read aloud. The first thing Kit said when he had finished
was, "Let's call Ray!"

It is an old adage with theatrical managers that "Shakespeare spells ruin"; but again Katharine Cornell was to
prove the falsity of an old theatrical maxim. "Romeo and
Juliet" played to packed houses.

Juliet Capulet was fourteen when she fell head over heels
in love with a young neighbor named Romeo Montague.
Playing the part in New York, Katharine Cornell was thirty-
six, yet even the most hardened critics thrilled to the youth
of her Juliet. She was Juliet—palpitant, exquisitely young,
gloriously and recklessly in love for the first time. There
were those who thought that as Elizabeth Barrett Katharine
Cornell had reached the zenith of her artistry, and that as
long as she lived she would never excel that role. These
same folk were now declaring the same thing in regard to
her Juliet.

According to John Mason Brown in the *New York Post*,
". . . The evening was an important one in Miss Cornell's
career. It came to New York audiences as a testing point
in her development as an actress . . . To say that she
emerged triumphantly from the evening both as an actress
and a manageress is but to state an agreeable truth, to add
that beyond any shadow of a doubt she is today 'The First

Lady' of our stage is but to state another of no less agreeable truth . . . Miss Cornell's Juliet is luscious and charming. It finds her at her mellowest and most glamorous. It
burns with the intensity Miss Cornell brings to all her
acting. It moves gracefully and lightly; is endlessly haunting
in its pictorial qualities; and reveals a Miss Cornell who
equals the beauty of the lyric lines she speaks with a new-
found lyric quality in her own voice . . ."

With the closing of "Romeo and Juliet," "The Barretts"
was revived for three weeks, and then rehearsals began for
"Flowers of the Forest," a play which Katharine Cornell
had chosen because of its strong plea for peace. On its tryout in Baltimore, the show had all the earmarks of success.
The opening night in New York, April 4th, it rained again,
and again the actors remembered hopefully the old adage
of the theater. But the play closed on May 11th, proving
that theatrical omens, like all other omens, often go awry.
"Flowers of the Forest" in the language of Broadway, was
a "flop."

After its closing Kit went directly to her beloved Garmisch and remained there the entire summer. She and
McClintic planned to revive "Romeo and Juliet" on tour
next season, then play it for two weeks in New York, and
follow it with Shaw's "Saint Joan." Her mind was now
engrossed with that character.

Henderson was eager for her to do Joan, and he, Kit,
McClintic, Gertrude Macy and Stanton Griffis all went to
Rouen to see the very spot where Joan had been burned
at the stake.

Wholeheartedly now, Kit set herself to get all possible

good out of the character of the heroic Maid of Domremy.
Not a single nuance must be overlooked. She must be fair
to the character she had chosen to portray, for only in this
way could she be fair with her audience and herself. In
order to accustom herself to Joan's boyish stride, she rehearsed in a riding habit. At the first rehearsals, listening
to her read the part, the actors declared among themselves:
"Cornell's going to be *terrible!*" But as day followed day,
Joan came to live and breathe within Katharine Cornell.
The actors watched a gradual development, a slow and
meticulous unfoldment, until at last, somewhat surprised,
they were whispering, "Why, she's going to be *marvelous*
in this part! She's the perfect Joan—her walk, her voice,
that up-flung challenge of her head!"

The play opened for its tryout in Buffalo, where Kit
caught a bad cold. By the time they reached Pittsburgh her
fever was high, and the doctor looked grave.

"It's the flu," he announced. "You can't possibly go on."

"You mean the New York opening will have to be postponed?"

"Absolutely."

She groaned. This was terrible, terrible. Not to open on
schedule—to lie here seven whole days! To feel oneself
prepared, ready for the New York opening—and then to
have to go to bed! She had not the *right*, she argued fret-
fully, to let herself take cold. There were certain obligations
one owed to one's calling—and the most important of these
was health. She had always taken the greatest care of her
health, but a poorly heated theater, a drafty stage in Buffalo
had taken their toll.

She lay now, fuming at this enforced idleness. Ray came

and, sitting by her bedside, sought to divert her with his talk of the world tour he wanted her to take someday. He had thought so much about it during their long association that he could even now discuss knowingly the places they would visit—Australia, New Zealand, Hawaii, China, Japan, the Malay States, Java, Siam, Burma, India, Egypt, Palestine, the Philippines, France, South Africa, Switzerland, Turkey, Greece, Italy, Austria, Hungary, Poland, Czechoslovakia, Russia, Finland, Sweden, Norway, Denmark, Holland, Belgium, the British Isles, Ireland, Mexico—and back to New York. This was his great dream.

"Dear Ray," she thought, appreciating his friendship, his kindliness, "what would we ever do without him?"

Gert came in, her arms laden with detective stories. "Here you are, Kit, these ought to ease the boredom a little. Oh, by the way, a newspaperwoman called me up. She's writing an article advising young people whether or not to go on the stage. She wants to know, quite frankly, what you would tell them."

"If I had a daughter," Katharine Cornell answered, "and she wanted to be an actress, I'd tell her this: 'Only try for a career on the stage if you are certain there is nothing else you could be happy in!'"

CHAPTER SIXTEEN

KATHARINE CORNELL GOES TO THE WHITE HOUSE

$\mathcal{S}$AINT JOAN" opened on March 9, 1936, at the Martin Beck Theater, New York City. Here was a Joan spirited, lovely, inspired, looking not a day over eighteen. Now and then theater-goers witness that which remains forever indelibly stamped upon their memories. These events are rare, these memories are beyond price. No one who ever saw Pavlova dance The Swan, who ever heard Kreisler play; no one who ever saw Henry Irving in "The Bells," Edwin Booth as "Hamlet," Bernhardt as "Camille," Charlotte Cushman as "Lady Macbeth," Joseph Jefferson as "Rip van Winkle" or Katharine Cornell as "Joan" was ever able to forget these performances. These were not merely evenings of entertainment—these were all unforgettable *experiences*.

With the ending of the New York run the play visited Boston, Philadelphia, Chicago, Los Angeles and San Francisco. It was during the playing of Saint Joan that the University of Wisconsin conferred the degree of Doctor of Letters upon Katharine Cornell, an occasion which, always shunning public appearances, she faced with considerable trepidation. It was not the first, nor would it be the last time the actress was to receive such honor. In 1935 she had been the recipient of the Chancellor's Medal from the University of Buffalo. This was the first time the medal was awarded to a woman and the first time for an artist; also in that year she had received the New York Drama League Award for her performance of Juliet, the medal being presented by that fine old man of the theater, Daniel Frohman.

Kit and Guthrie had planned to spend their vacation again in Majorca that summer following the close of "Saint Joan," but the outbreak of the Spanish Civil War necessitated a change in plan, and instead they went for awhile to a rented camp in Martha's Vineyard. Here, carefree in slacks and sweater, Kit wandered along the beach, the dogs frisking about her. In her strolls she found a spot—a spot even lovelier than Garmisch, a place which she knew at once she had to make her very own. They still owned their town house in Beekham Place, and Sneden's Landing which was delightful for week-ends, but here was the ideal place for a summer home. Joyously, she and McClintic discussed it. Both agreed that here on this island was everything they wanted. Here was ruggedness, beauty, isolation. Here were tall, stately pines swaying restfully in the salt breeze. Here were the dunes, spectral in the moonlight—and here was the sea.

"We'll build our house right at the water's edge," Kit exclaimed enthusiastically, "and we'll have loads of fireplaces!"

"And pine walls and pine furniture—"

"And big, square chimneys and a roof that slopes—"

"And windows—huge windows—as many as we can get!"

So they planned, and presently they were silent, merged with that singular silence about them. They relaxed, feeling already at home, content, just letting that balmlike stillness flow into and through them.

They returned to Garmisch that year for a single month, which was all the time they could spare since rehearsals were already scheduled for "The Wingless Victory," a new play by Maxwell Anderson which would have its opening in Washington in late November.

The part of Oparre, the Malay Princess, was utterly different from any character Katharine Cornell had ever portrayed. The scene of the play was laid in New England in 1800. As "Flowers of the Forest" had been a plea for peace, "The Wingless Victory" was a plea for tolerance and understanding between the white and yellow races. The play, which opened in New York at the Empire Theater on December 13, 1936, was a success almost equaling that of "Saint Joan." It ran at the Empire for one hundred and eight performances, and in March, 1937, it was produced in conjunction with "Candida," which held the boards for Wednesday matinees as well as Monday and Saturday nights.

How much of victory had Katharine Cornell herself known in her thirty-nine years! Never once had she compromised in regard to her art. Professional jealousy was unknown to her. Always she had believed that the play was paramount, and had never failed to surround herself with the best casts available. Her mail was enormous; letters of praise and criticism, letters begging interviews, soliciting her patronage for organizations, begging advice as to how to go on the stage, asking that she endorse face creams or cigarettes, letters begging for money, requests for autographs. She was still an essentially modest person, a characteristic shared in common with two other dominant figures of the theater—Henry Irving and Edwin Booth. As people meeting those two were invariably impressed with their modesty and gentleness, so were those who now met Katharine Cornell.

She was still ardently interested in athletics—skating, tennis, golf. She used almost no make-up on the street and as little as possible on the stage; as for jewelry, she wore none, not even a wedding ring.

The radio had no appeal for her, and she listened to it only to hear the concerts. Movies and crime stories were still her only dissipations. She smoked only when on vacations between plays, and was rigidly abstemious as to drinking. Parties and shopping were things to be avoided whenever possible; either Gertrude Macy or Eveline bought all her clothes. She had a way of saying to her friends, "I like those shoes you're wearing. Where did you get them?" and when she had received the answer, she would ask, "Do you mind if I send Eveline to get me a pair?" Dieting was never necessary as she was naturally slender. She was five feet six and a half inches tall, and weighed one hundred and thirty pounds.

For the past ten years her career had been firmly established. The world had given her everything, even more than she had asked of it. At thirty-nine her art, like her physical beauty, had been enriched in its maturity; each succeeding year had brought greater depth of understanding, a revitalization of her acting ability, a more *glowing* quality.

That this fact was universally recognized was proven

on March 31, 1937. "The Wingless Victory" was still
running, but it was necessary to close the theater for one
night to enable Katharine Cornell to go to Washington
and receive a medal. Each year the Chi Omega National
Sorority chooses an American woman whose achievements
are considered worthy of this honor. In 1937 the National
Achievement Award was given to Katharine Cornell and
the place of its presentation was the White House.

When Kit heard of it she simply stared. "To—me?" she
queried.

Gert smiled and nodded.

That such an honor had come to her amazed Kit almost
to speechlessness. She had never considered herself a great
actress, but she was too fundamentally honest to pretend
that receiving this distinction did not please her. When
Gertrude outlined to her the ceremony which would accompany the presentation of the medal, her eyes took on
the expression of a fawn startled in the forest. The feeling
of sheer terror at the prospect shot like a bolt through every
nerve of her body.

"I shall never be able to go through with it," she murmured.

Gert said: "Of course you will," with confidence; for she
knew that Kit Cornell could and would go through with
anything that she had to do.

"You'll be called upon for a speech," Gert told her.

"Oh, dear!" gasped Kit, and fear became a paralyzing
thing.

But neither Gertrude Macy, Ray Henderson nor Guthrie
McClintic were apprehensive, although they knew how
difficult it would be for her. She wrote out her speech, a

very short and simple one, and after they had all approved of it, set herself to memorize it.

Mrs. Roosevelt had written asking for the names of Kit's closest associates and friends so that they might be invited, and Kit had sent back a list which included—Ray Henderson, Gertrude Macy, and Conger Goodyear.

By the time the curtain rang down Monday night, Kit's nerves were taut. Tomorrow was the big event. "I'll just never be able to go *through* with it," she kept saying.

Next morning at breakfast she found herself without appetite. It was suddenly difficult to swallow. McClintic was calm, smiling, patient, saying little. As the party boarded the train at eleven o'clock, he noticed that she was carrying six books.

"What's the library for?" he asked amusedly.

"Detective stories," she explained. "I thought it would take my mind off things if I read on the way down."

They sat there in the train, talking little. Each of them had brought one bag. Kit's was smart, neat. McClintic's was a battered and disreputable thing. He had had it for years. It had gone with him everywhere, all over Europe, all over America. For a long time now it had shown signs of protesting under the strain, but McClintic, being a loyal soul, clung to it manfully.

When the train stopped at Washington, a White House employee met them. He was grave and somewhat on the pompous side, and as he turned to lead them to the Presidential car, Guthrie's bag took this inopportune time to burst open. The Washington station was suddenly strewn with BVDs and other intimate articles of masculine apparel. Even now, as everybody scrambled for socks, ties,

shirts, shoes and dress suit, McClintic's poise did not desert
him. The things were stuffed pell-mell into the bag again
and the party proceeded to the car. The presentation was
not to be made until after dinner that evening, and as the
limousine drew closer and closer to the White House, Kit
sat wondering miserably how she would ever be able to
live that long.

But her hostess knew how to put guests at their ease.
Eleanor Roosevelt had seen "The Wingless Victory" twice,
and in her column, "My Day," had commented upon
Katharine Cornell's superb acting. The First Lady of
America was an ardent theater-goer. Informal, charming,
she is one of the friendliest people in the world. Katharine
Cornell felt the warmth of that friendliness the minute she
stepped into the Blue Room where the President and Mrs.
Roosevelt were having tea with Lord and Lady Tweedsmuir
(who had arrived as representatives of the British Crown),
and Secretary and Mrs. Cordell Hull.

Everything was delightfully unstilted and affable about
the tea table that day, and Kit's panic began to abate a
trifle. Talk flowed easily, wittily, and the atmosphere of
hominess was both soothing and stimulating. The President
was fifty-five, a big man with massive shoulders. Despite
the hatred and bitterness of strong opposing factions, he
had been re-elected the year before by a majority so vast
as to testify to the trust of the people. Cordell Hull was
sixty-six. Already these two were keeping a watchful eye
upon Germany where an overbearing, power-lusting
Fuehrer was telling his followers that they were a master
race, destined to rule the world. All this was dangerous,
all this was perilously reminiscent of 1914 when, under the

Kaiser, Germans had been taught that they were superior to every race on earth. But none of this darkened the pleasant conversation which flowed about that hospitable tea table on the late afternoon of March 30, 1937.

Watching his wife, McClintic saw her relaxing, saw that quick, brilliant smile come and go, saw the tranquillity of the well-shaped, ringless hands. They were closely akin in spirit, these two. The busy, tempestuous years had welded them together even closer, each the perfect complement of the other. They had been married now sixteen years, sixteen years of achievement, of devotion to high ideals. Life had been good to them both. Together they had shared their triumphs, together they had faced their rare failures. It had been a good life, they would not have exchanged it for another. Now, here they were in the White House, together still, Kit about to receive a much-coveted honor—and to Guthrie McClintic it all seemed very *right*.

Presently the group about the tea table was breaking up to dress for dinner and the presentation of the medal which would come afterward. Mr. and Mrs. McClintic were shown to their room.

Already their things were unpacked. Beginning to dress, Kit was very quiet. Understanding her so well, McClintic said nothing, but he knew that the more quiet she became, the greater was the tension under which she labored. Her full, generous mouth had a drawn, tight look, her dark eyes were unnaturally bright, and he knew that the panic of the morning had returned with the force of an avalanche. Distractedly, secretly, she was telling herself again: "I shall never be able to go through with it." She tried to divert her mind by attempting to recall the short speech of ac-

ceptance she had learned, and in the midst of this, she
became aware of the fact that Guthrie seemed to be
frantically searching for something. In answer to her question, he replied forlornly, "My collar button."

"Oh, dear. It must be there. You certainly wouldn't have
come to Washington without collar buttons!"

"Of course I wouldn't. I know they were packed, but I've
hunted through everything four times and they're just not
there!"

"Wait. I'll look."

But after a further hurried search, the dreadful truth was
evident that Guthrie McClintic, New York's famous director, had no collar button. This was serious. Obviously he
could not appear without a collar button. Moments were
passing. Collar buttons had suddenly become the most
important things in the world.

"They must have been lost when your bag burst open at
the station."

McClintic, who had been thinking the same thing,
nodded, remarked that that did not help matters, and gave
a swift, apprehensive glance at the clock. He felt a sharp
sense of guilt for having lost his collar button, rather like
a little boy who has been sent to the grocer's and returns
minus the most essential item of his errand. Again they
searched, and again the search was fruitless.

"There's nothing to do," decided Kit, "but to tell Mrs.
Roosevelt about it."

"Good heavens! Bother Mrs. Roosevelt about my collar
button?"

But Kit had already rung the bell. "It will be all right,"
she told him, and forced herself to smile.

"You rang, Madam?" asked a dignified, middle-aged maid.

"Yes. Will you please tell Mrs. Roosevelt that—that we're terribly sorry but Mr. McClintic has lost his collar buttons!"

Presently the maid was back. Mrs. Roosevelt had sent two collar buttons. McClintic breathed easily. Now everything was all right.

"Do you suppose they belong to the President?" he asked with a grin, when the door had closed upon the maid.

"Probably," answered his wife, who wanted to forget collar buttons.

She had acquired for the occasion a stunning new white gown. It was intricately cut and its intricacies included its fastening. With this, for a time, she struggled.

"Could I help?" asked McClintic, at last.

"I'm afraid you'll have to. I thought I knew how this thing fastened, but—"

Again his gaze sought the clock, and manfully he set to work on the dress. Brilliant in directing his companies, McClintic was at a loss when it came to deciphering the fastening on his wife's gown. He grunted—and kept on.

"We'll be late for dinner," Kit announced tragically.

She was only telling Guthrie that which he was already fearing. It seemed inevitable now that they would be late. Her distracted eyes sought the beautiful corsage of orchids which the President had sent her, and she murmured imploringly, "Please hurry!"

This request seemed a bit pointless to Guthrie, whose face by now was white. "How the devil—" his voice sounded breathless. but he continued his struggles, and at length, in complete exasperation, he cried, "Oh, for God's sake, get a safety pin!"

The advice seemed the only solution at that dreadful moment. Kit rang the bell again. Her voice was steady as she asked the maid for a safety pin. These, also, it seemed, could be had at the White House. At long last the dress was pinned, and the orchids were on her shoulder.

Downstairs the guests were already in line and at the moment when Katharine Cornell and Guthrie McClintic took their places, a footman announced the entrance of the President and Mrs. Roosevelt, and Lord and Lady Tweedsmuir. The line moved forward to greet them. Mrs. Roosevelt, beautifully poised, was smiling at everyone as if they were all good friends and she loved having them there.

Kit scarcely knew what she ate that night at the White House dinner. Now and then her eyes would meet those of her old friend, Alexander Woollcott, who was smiling at her and who seemed to be enjoying himself hugely. Ray, looking scholarly and distinguished in his dinner clothes, flashed her a glance that was fond and encouraging.

Dinner over, everyone except the President went to the East Room where a page assigned them to their seats. The ballroom was almost filled with six hundred guests. There would be speeches. The members of the committee of the award were present. Mrs. August Belmont, Woollcott, Mrs. Laura Gardin Fraser, representing the Field of Art on the committee of the Award, presided.

Kit's hands were icy. Desperately she tried to remember the short speech she had prepared. She had said it smoothly to Gert only yesterday, but now not a word could she recall.

Her mind was in a state of utter chaos. People were saying splendid things about her. The moment for the presentation of the medal was approaching, and she was more and more distrustful of her knees. The audience was smiling appreciatively at Woollcott's speech. He was telling them all about the time when they were on their way to Seattle and the train had been held up because of floods. ". . . so the curtain was rung up," went on Woollcott, still beaming upon them all, "and they were allowed to see the wheels go 'round . . ."

How, Kit was asking herself, shall I have the strength to rise when they call me to give me the medal? And how did the speech begin?

Mrs. Fraser was now introducing Mrs. Roosevelt. How calm and happy everyone seemed! Perhaps of everyone present only Kit's friends and Mrs. Roosevelt knew what the guest of honor was undergoing. Mrs. Roosevelt *must* have sensed Kit's agony for, always wise and considerate, she was saying, ". . . I hope that while Miss Cornell probably wishes now that she might have this evening only as a memory, that she will also carry away the feeling that she has had a happy time, because we, all of us here tonight, many of us just playgoers, would like to give back to her some of the pleasure she has given us . . . You have served your art and served the people and tonight I give you this medal in gratitude that it can go to you, and that tonight's National Achievement Award is given in a field which I consider so valuable to the country. I am grateful also to you as a woman and an artist who has done much to bring a realization of her art to the people. My congratulations!"

They were applauding. Kit had risen. She was not an actress now. Tremblingly, haltingly, she began to speak. It was not the speech she had prepared.

"I—I—n-nothing that has ever—happened to me has—has—been quite so—so moving, so—so—"

It was Mrs. Roosevelt who, realizing the drama of the moment, laughingly put her arm about that white, quivering figure, and brought the meeting to a close.

Now that it was over, Katharine Cornell stepped down from the platform suddenly at ease. It was over. People crowded about, shaking hands, and she laughed back at them.

"Have you got the medal?" asked Woollcott.

"Oh, heavens! I left it up there on the platform!"

"That," McClintic told her solemnly, "is what might be called the perfect touch!"

In his study, the President dimly heard the voices below at the reception which followed, but when it was over his door opened and there were his wife, Lord and Lady Tweedsmuir, the McClintics and their party.

They sat around informally and talked, and the President gave one of his spontaneous, hearty laughs when someone told him that Kit had been so excited that she had left her medal on the platform. Now she was having a lovely time, expanding under the warmth and hospitality of the Roosevelts and the quiet friendliness of the Tweedsmuirs. At long last she was really beginning to enjoy herself.

Finally this, too, was over, and the McClintics were back in their room, packing. They had been invited to spend the night at the White House, but because the theater had been closed for only one performance and Kit would have

to give a show the following night, Kit, McClintic, Gert
and Ray decided to take the late train to New York.

"Have a good time, Kit?"

"Lovely!" she replied, and her very voice sounded radiant.

Looking as bright as when the evening began, Mrs.
Roosevelt came into the room, cozily chatting until the
packing was finished, and they were told that the car was
waiting to take them to the station.

As the car drove away from the White House, Kit leaned
back and closed her eyes while a host of pleasant memories
crowded into her mind. The President and his kindliness;
Mrs. Roosevelt and the spontaneity of her warmth, the
richness of her understanding, the beauty of her zest for
life; Alec Woollcott and his *savoir-faire*; the Tweedsmuirs
and their simplicity; the eloquence of Mrs. Belmont;
Guthrie and his patience, his ability to feel at home anywhere; Gert, wise and clever and loyal; Ray, lanky and
efficient.

"Tired, Kit?" asked Gert.

"No. It just suddenly came to me how much, how very
much I have to be grateful for!"

CHAPTER SEVENTEEN

THE HOME AMONG THE DUNES

ECAUSE IT was situated beyond the two head-lines, West Chop and East Chop, Kit called the house at Martha's Vineyard, "Chip Chop." A Chop means a point of land with a light on it and that is what Chip Chop is— a point of land from which, out at sea, can be seen the light of the McClintic summer home. The squat, sprawling house, simple in construction, faces the water, while all about it on the three remaining sides are low scrub oaks and the wildness of the dunes. It is a frame house, really three houses strung together, with broad and conspicuous white stone chimneys. Inside, the rooms are airy, uncrowded and spacious. One room, the room with the grand piano, contains two fireplaces, a ping-pong table and a real Bavarian tile stove. The walls and furniture are of unpainted pine, and there are multitudinous windows. There is a large outdoor fireplace where the McClintics often cook their dinners, barbecue style. Chip Chop has every convenience except a telephone.

Katharine Cornell rises each morning at 8:30 and five minutes later is swimming in the sea. Next she feeds the chickens and has breakfast. Days are full to the brim. After breakfast there is the planting of flowers, as well as the watering of the flowers, the shrubs and vines which she has already planted. Next, there is driftwood to be gathered for the fireplaces, and the marketing to do.

Clad in denim slacks or overalls or dungarees and a worn sweater, she spends the days almost entirely out of doors. She knows the butcher by his first name, and exchanges recipes with the competent island housewives to whom she is not a great actress, but simply a good neighbor. Here she cooks, trying out new recipes, discovering what each guest likes and preparing it herself. Here, too, there is time for reading, and, usually at sundown, she takes long walks on the lonely beach, the dogs—Leif, Luni, Illo and Biscuit—at her heels. Flush had died in 1937 at seven years of age at Sneden's Landing. He had loved being an actor, and they had buried him tenderly at Sneden's, wrapped in an actor's coat.

Katharine Cornell walks with a free, calm stride, letting the wind have its will with her dark, fine hair. Returning home, she indulges in a comparatively new-found hobby, that of refinishing old furniture—an interest shared with her neighbor, James Cagney.

It was this informality, this freedom, this quietude of Chip Chop that she wanted as the long, hard season of "Wingless Victory" continued. She was tired, inexpressibly tired. Suddenly everything required a gigantic effort. She could look back upon more than twenty years of almost incessant work. Even the so-called vacations were never real holidays, for she had invariably carried a manuscript along with her, and there was always a production to plan, a part to study.

Knowing that she was not only losing her splendid vitality but her interest in her work, Ray watched her anxiously.

"This isn't like you. What's the matter?"

"I don't know, Ray. Nothing. Everything. Me. Life. I'm suddenly at cross-purposes with myself. I don't know where I'm going. I don't know what it's all about. Sometimes I think I'd like to stop—just stop; just give up—retire—I don't know."

A look of dismay crossed his honest, good-natured face.

"Oh, no! No, don't say that!"

"But I mean it. I—"

"No, don't think of it, don't even speak of it. You can't stop. You mustn't. There's so much ahead."

"For instance?"

"Well, there's the tour. There's the world tour we've talked about so often."

She smiled at him affectionately. "You'd love that, wouldn't you, Ray?"

"Love it—yes; but most of all, I want it—for you. All around the world, you and the company. And the world will see what America has to give in the way of the theater. And it's practical! It could pay for itself, I know it could."

He was worried about her, and wretched. It hurt to know that Ray was unhappy because of her. Later, alone with her husband, the memory of Ray's face haunting her, she said: "I'm making Ray terribly unhappy. I hate that."

"I know. It's because he's so fond of you. Fonder of you, perhaps, than anybody in his world."

"His world is very large. It takes in the whole globe. All these years we've been talking about a world tour. I think Ray wants that more than anything. For years it has been his dream. Well, why not? Why not go on this tour as he wants us to?"

"You mean go just because Ray wants it so badly?"

"Yes. I really think I mean just that. Isn't that as good a reason as any? If it will make him happy then I believe it is probably the right thing to do. And why shouldn't we do it? We'll go anywhere, everywhere he wants us to go. He's such a precious friend. Ever since he came with us we've relied on him and followed his advice."

"All right, Kit. We'll let Ray start ahead as soon as he wants to. If, after looking the European situation over, he feels that the time isn't propitious or the scheme isn't practical, we can postpone it. Anyhow, there's one thing sure—we can trust to Ray's judgment."

Henderson was overjoyed when they told him of their acquiescence. He labored happily over plans. Every detail had to be worked out beforehand. He was naturally an orderly person, and besides, he was determined that everything must be made as easy for Kit as possible. He would go ahead, of course, and make all arrangements. His mind teemed with ideas. He sailed in early May, 1937.

"The Wingless Victory" continued its run for some months longer, and when at last it closed, Gertrude and Guthrie found it impossible to leave New York. Longing for her house by the sea, Kit went to Martha's Vineyard alone. Ray's letters and cables had at first been enthusiastic, but as his voyaging progressed, he found conditions everywhere sadly unsettled. Farsighted, he realized that to undertake the tour at this time might be hazardous. There was so much he wanted to tell Kit which could not be said in letters and cables. He wanted to get back now, wanted to

stretch his long legs at ease on the wide veranda at Chip
Chop and tell her all about everything.

On Friday, October 1st, a telegraph boy brought her a
cable. It was from Henderson and had been sent from
Cairo. "Egypt keen flying London tomorrow love Ray."

That afternoon the Cagneys, with Mr. and Mrs. Denys
Wortman, also neighbors, arrived for a visit. The five of
them sat on the veranda talking about the contemplated
tour.

"Ray's one of the best friends Guthrie and I have ever
had," Kit said. "He has been with us for over six years. I
don't know what we'd do without Ray. Here's a cable I got
from him only this morning." She passed it to Cagney.

"Oh, he's already in London. I suppose he'll be home
soon?" he asked.

"Yes, it won't be long now. He's really on his way back.
Dear Ray." There was the sound of a plane overhead, and
her eyes followed it, watching it as it landed upon the lake.
"Wouldn't it be wonderful if that were Ray?" she asked.

They all laughed, for of course it was absurd, since only
a few hours previously she had received a cable from him
from Cairo. All day she thought about Ray, wanting to
talk to him. The next morning her mind was still focused
upon him, not worriedly but tenderly, longing to see him.
It amazed her when Gert and Guthrie arrived. She had not
known they were coming, and she ran to meet them eagerly.

"Have you heard anything from Ray?" she asked.

"We've had a cable—" Gert began, and then stopped.

"From the American Consulate at Athens," added Mc-
Clintic.

"The—American Consulate? Athens? Why—what—"

"You'd better read it," answered her husband.

Kit took the paper. "Henderson trapped and drowned in submerged seaplane," she read.

She sank into a convenient chair, staring at them. Gert's eyes were frankly wet now, and she took off her glasses to wipe the tears away.

Kit spoke quietly. "I can't believe it. It can't be true. Not Ray."

It was a grief which touched them all. They were stunned, silent. None of them could conceive of the fact that they would never see Ray Henderson again.

"It can't be true," she kept saying dazedly.

"He always loved flying," McClintic murmured.

And again they were silent.

By 1938 it was clear to all of them that conditions in Europe would make the contemplated tour impossible. According to Henderson's plan the tour was to have started that spring. Since this plan must now be abandoned, Katharine Cornell decided to take a "sabbatical" year.

A whole year in which she could go anywhere she wanted to go, do anything she wanted to do, go to bed when she wanted to—a year of complete freedom, a year in which to think things out. She stayed at Martha's Vineyard until Thanksgiving, after which she and her husband made a hurried pleasure trip abroad, getting home just in time for Christmas. The rest of the winter was spent between the Beekman Place house and the place at Sneden's Landing.

That tranquil year away from the theater gave her what she needed. Her body became recharged with vitality, her zest for work returned. There were plays to read for the forthcoming season—both new plays and old. One must plan carefully, choose carefully. Since she had been under her own management she had never starred herself, and she had never produced a play in which she did not have implicit faith.

In the spring of 1939 she took "Herod and Marianne" on the road for four weeks, but the play was thought unsuitable for New York, and "No Time for Comedy" was put into rehearsal to open April 17, 1939. Though this was lighter in vein than any play Katharine Cornell had ever produced, the public liked it, and its run continued for over a year, closing at last on May 15, 1940, after another transcontinental tour playing fifty-six cities in twenty-nine states, and covering well over fifteen thousand miles.

Katharine Cornell went on the air this year for the first time at the opening of the annual Red Cross drive in a radio presentation of "The Barretts of Wimpole Street." Guthrie McClintic was the director and introduced the scenes, and Brian Aherne flew from California to play opposite her again in his old part of the charming, debonair Robert Browning.

As the world was at war again, Garmisch was out of the question that summer, but while at Chip Chop Kit planned a revival of Shaw's "The Doctor's Dilemma." The scene was laid in 1900, and people who saw it said that never had Katharine Cornell looked more lovely than she did now, in costumes inspired by Baldini's paintings. Like its predecessor the play was a hit, its run lasting from February to December of 1941.

It was during the run of this play that Katharine Cornell

gave the first five-cent matinee for children. The house was packed with youngsters that Saturday afternoon of May 31st. Actors, theater attachés, stagehands, all donated their services. It was one of the most appreciative audiences to which the actors had ever played. When it was over, about twenty children were permitted backstage for a visit with the star, while over four hundred waited outside the stage door for a glimpse of her.

She was playing San Francisco in "The Doctor's Dilemma" when the Axis powers declared war on the United States. On her way to the theater one night the first air alarm sounded, and suddenly the city was plunged into its initial blackout. All traffic stopped. People were grim and quiet—waiting. Who knew? At any moment Jap planes might come, blasting away at the city as only a month ago they had poured destruction upon Honolulu. Katharine Cornell knew only one thing—that whether the Japs came or not, she had to give a show. She went stumbling through the pitch darkness of the streets, guiding herself warily by touching the buildings with her outstretched hands, and finally reached the theater. Though there were only two hundred people in the auditorium, the show went on.

"Rose Burke," which followed "The Doctor's Dilemma," had only an eight weeks' run. The success or failure of a play seemed now an infinitesimal thing compared to the stupendous drama of a world at war. The thought uppermost in Kit's mind those days was: *What can I do to help my country win?*

In times of stress it is always the actors who are among the first to respond. Vast sums to help the war effort could be raised through the theaters. The question was only: What was the speediest and best way for Katharine Cornell to help?

She lost no time in assembling an all-star cast for a revival of "Candida," the receipts to go to the Army and Navy Relief Fund. The brilliant cast included Katharine Cornell, Raymond Massey, Burgess Meredith, Dudley Digges, Mildred Naturck and Stanley Bell, all of whom gladly gave their services. In thirty-five performances the play grossed one hundred and twenty-two thousand, two hundred and forty-seven dollars and fifty cents. It closed in Washington where, after the final performance, the company was entertained at dinner by Mrs. Roosevelt.

Kit had been back in New York only a short time when one day in the Beekman Place house, as she entered the library from puttering among the shrubs on the terrace, McClintic called out to her asking if she had ever read Anton Chekov's "The Three Sisters."

"Yes," she answered. "I read it a long time ago. Why?"

"Well, I've just finished it. Don't read it again until I can read it with you!"

And when he had read it to her, they both knew that here was their next production. They considered it a truly great play, and they set about at once to provide it with a peerless cast.

There were those who advised against it, thinking it a peculiar play for Kit Cornell to choose since the role she would play was not, strictly speaking, a star part. The burden of the play rested upon four women, each part equal in length and importance. For these parts she might have chosen three women of such inferior acting ability as to make herself stand out; but instead, in casting the other three feminine roles, she chose the most accomplished actresses she could find. Olga was played by Judith Anderson, long a star in her own right; Irina was played by Gertrude Musgrove, and Natasha by Ruth Gordon. Only someone familiar with the stage could fully appreciate the generosity of this gesture.

The play itself, written forty-two years ago, and first produced in Moscow in 1901, is a dismal story of the futility and frustration which engulfed the upper classes in Russia prior to the revolution.

Rehearsals were scheduled to begin October 5, 1942. Woollcott often dropped in to watch them, and expressing his admiration and enthusiasm for the production, repeatedly affirmed that it was bound to be a success. On November 30th the show had its tryout in Washington, Baltimore and Philadelphia, reaching the Ethel Barrymore Theater in New York on December 19th. Kit's abiding faith in the play was justified, for despite the fact that from time to time it had been produced previously and had never been an outstanding success, it now drew capacity houses for one hundred and twenty-three performances until April 3rd, when it began a limited tour which included Boston, Buffalo, Toronto, Detroit, Cleveland, Pittsburgh, Chicago. The final performance in New York was given in aid of the Russian War Relief. During the engagement in Chicago, which ended in June, 1943, a special Thursday matinee was given for the benefit of The Actors' Fund of America, of which Katharine Cornell had been re-elected vice-president in May.

In November, 1942, she went on the air for the second

time. She had refused the enormous sums which were constantly being offered by the broadcasting companies because she felt that radio required its own technique, but the Red Cross needed help now as it had never needed it before, and so she made an exception, not for personal gain, but to help her fellow-man.

The year 1943 brought her one real sorrow. Her friend, Alexander Woollcott, was suddenly stricken with a heart condition while broadcasting, and he died next day at the hospital. It was a shock to all his friends, and Katharine Cornell felt a great personal loss.

Demands upon her now were almost incessant. Never had she been busier. In February, through her efforts, "The Three Sisters" became a braille book. On Sunday afternoon, March 21st, she made another radio appearance, again for the Red Cross, in an appeal for nurses' aides. America heard a beautifully modulated voice and perfect diction, a magnetic voice, charged with profound sincerity. On Thursday, March 24th, she gave a special matinee for the benefit of the Red Cross, which was then in the midst of its drive to raise funds. In April, Wheeler Williams, the sculptor, was making a bust of her in aid of the Red Cross Fund, and in addition to all this, there was her work at the Stage Door Canteen.

The Stage Door Canteen, though it meant strenuous work, was fun. This was a jolly, friendly place, established strictly for enlisted men. No officer and no civilian was served, but the servicemen crowded into the place. There was no charge for anything, and the food was handed out to them by the most famous actresses in America. Twenty-three hundred actors were volunteers to help operate the canteen. Some cooked, some sliced bread, others buttered it, some washed dishes, some wiped off tables, some carried trays, others gave impromptu entertainment, but one and all they worked, and they worked joyously. With Alfred Lunt, Lynn Fontanne, Helen Hayes, and other celebrities, Katharine Cornell washed dishes, handed out doughnuts and poured coffee. This brought about her movie debut, for it was decided that the activities of the canteen would be filmed in order to raise more money for war relief.

Even though she would appear briefly in the film, she was told that there would have to be a test. On the morning of the event, Kit phoned Gertrude Macy at the Cornell-McClintic office in Rockefeller Center.

"Gert," she announced, "the test is this afternoon."

"Yes," answered Gert, composedly.

"Well, I haven't a thing to wear!"

Gert smiled, thinking to herself fondly that it was just like Kit not to think of clothes until the morning of the test. But Gert simply hung up the phone, put on her hat, walked over to Hattie Carnegie's and chose two dresses.

To Kit, it was strange having men come to make her up. It was strange, too, all that fussing with the lights. She had consented to appear in the talkie because she considered it her duty to help in any way she could, even though she had expected it to be a terrifying experience. How often had she heard her friends discussing something they called "camera fright" which, they assured her knowingly, was ten times worse than stage fright! But to her surprise she actually enjoyed the occasion. Always before she had said: "I may make a picture someday—at the right time and in the right role." This was the time—when her country needed the money; this was the right role—serving the men who were about to risk their lives that that country might endure.

During the run of "The Three Sisters" she was still spending her week-ends at Sneden's Landing, driving in to New York in a station wagon filled with dogs. She was forty-five in February, 1943. Many colleges had honored her. In addition to receiving the Chancellor's Medal from the University of Buffalo, she had received the degree of Doctor of Letters from the University of Wisconsin, Elmira College, Smith College, Hobart College, and the University of Pennsylvania in 1938, which was followed in 1941 by the degree of Doctor of Fine Arts from Clark University.

When "The Three Sisters" was closing, people kept asking her what play she intended to do next. She told them honestly that she did not know. For a long time now she had been wanting to produce an all-star revival of Shakespeare's "Antony and Cleopatra"—perhaps, she said, it would be that, or perhaps that would come later.

No, she did not know exactly what she would do, but it was enough for the present just to know that when the short tour of "The Three Sisters" ended, Chip Chop would be waiting, serene and kindly, in the midst of a worried, war-tossed world. This year she purchased a lovely meadow near the property, which she planned to farm. She moved on to it an old barn where she could keep a cow and a horse, and with her chickens, she hoped that soon the place would become self-sustaining. Perhaps another year she could arrange to get a couple of pigs and gradually acquire a complete farm and all that went with it.

But days at the home among the dunes were only pleasant

interludes, for inevitably there would come—again and again—that dynamic moment when for a time the world and its tempests are forgotten; that glorious, wonder-filled moment when from somewhere beyond the dressing-room door a voice would cry out those three ever-thrilling words: *"Curtain going up!"*

INDEX